THE KGB

By Don Lawson

A Wanderer Book
Published by Simon & Schuster Inc., New York

Designed by Prairie Graphics

Manufactured in the United States of America

10 9 8 7 6 5 4 3 2 1

WANDERER and colophon are registered trademarks
of Simon & Schuster, Inc.
SPY SHELF BOOKS is a trademark
of Simon & Schuster, Inc.
Also available in Julian Messner Library edition.

Library of Congress Cataloging in Publication Data

Lawson, Don.
  The KGB.

  (The Spy shelf)
  Bibliography; p.
  Includes index.
  1. Soviet Union. Komitet gosudarstvennoĭ bezopasnosti
—History. I. Title. II. Title: K.G.B. III. Series.
UB271.R9L33   1984   327.1′2′0947   83-14619
ISBN 0-671-46774-3
ISBN 0-671-50833-4 (lib. bdg.)

Table of Contents

Suburban
Spy Nest

IN THE SPRING of 1982, Americans were startled when the mayor of a New York City suburb declared: "We have an estate right in the middle of our community that is being used by the Russians for espionage—to eavesdrop on many of the defense industries on Long Island."

The statement was made by Alan Parante, mayor of Glen Cove, Long Island. The thirty-six-acre estate he referred to was known as Killenworth. On the estate was a forty-nine-room mansion used, the Russians claimed, as a weekend retreat for their diplomats working at the United Nations in New York City.

But Mayor Parante and the other town officials of Glen Cove claimed that the Russians were doing much more than relaxing at Killenworth.

They pointed out that the roof of the isolated mansion was filled with the kind of antennas used in high-powered electronic surveillance. They also pointed out that the mansion was on a high hill and well within range of telephone microwave relay towers. In addition, the estate was patrolled by armed guards and fierce guard dogs—to prevent the spies from being spied upon.

The Glen Cove officials' claims were immediately supported by a former Russian United Nations representative. He was Arkady Shevchenko, who had earlier defected to the United States. Shevchenko said that the Killenworth mansion had long been used to spy on the Grumman Aerospace Corporation as well as other defense contractors and high-technology industries.

"The federal government should demand that the Russians stop their spy activities at Killenworth," Mayor Parante later said, "or they should be thrown out."

When the United States took no action, Glen Cove officials took matters into their own hands. They revoked all of the beach passes that had been issued to the Russian diplomats. They also barred the Soviets from the local golf course and tennis courts.

These moves brought a reaction from the U. S. State Department—but the reaction was not against the alleged Soviet spy activity; it was against the Glen Cove officials.

A State Department spokesman pointed out that the Russians at Killenworth had diplomatic immunity and urged Glen Cove to stop meddling in foreign affairs. Unless Glen Cove officials retreated, the spokesman said, the Russians would retaliate against American diplomats in Moscow and Moscow's suburbs.

Unmoved, Mayor Parante responded by suggesting that the Russian UN diplomats be allowed to do their swimming in New York's Hudson River—not the cleanest of world waterways.

Russians Retaliate

Soviet officials in Moscow were not long in retaliating. They did ban employees of the U. S. embassy from using a Moscow River beach—a muddy recreation area that not many Soviet citizens found appealing. Soviet workers also refused to install plumbing in a new cottage at the U. S. embassy's weekend retreat outside Moscow.

Pravda, the official newspaper of the Soviet Union's Communist party, also rose to the occasion. It blamed U. S. President Ronald Reagan for creating an "anti-Soviet psychosis" that had infected all American citizens and especially those at Glen Cove. *Pravda* went on to claim that "double-dyed, delirious anti-Sovietism sits in official Washington and gives the American people nightmares."

In an effort to find a way out of this particular diplomatic nightmare, the U. S. State Department finally requested that Mayor Parante come to Washington for a conference. At this conference it became clear that Glen Cove officials not only objected to the presence of a Soviet spy nest in their midst, but they also objected to the fact that the Russians did not have to pay any property taxes on the Killenworth estate. Again because of diplomatic immunity, Glen Cove was being deprived of an annual $100,000 tax bill that would normally be collected on the Killenworth mansion and grounds. Mayor Parante suggested that Representative John LeBoutillier, one of Long Island's Republican congressmen, "introduce a bill into Congress that would reimburse small communities like Glen Cove for property taxes lost to exempt foreign-owned properties in their midst."

But the prospect for the passage of such a bill seemed dim—and so did the prospect of ending the battle between the citizens of Glen Cove and the Soviet spy-diplomats at Killenworth.

That there *were* Russian spies on the Glen Cove estate there could be no doubt. These spies were members of the twin Soviet intelligence services—the KGB and the GRU. What was also a fact, but was not widely known, was that the United States was paying a large part of these agents' salaries.

II

Soviet Spies in the United Nations

THE KGB IS OFFICIALLY known in the Soviet Union as the State Committee for Security (*Komitat Gosudarstvennoi Bezopastnosti*). Actually, the KGB is a huge Russian secret police force, which operates both inside and outside the borders of the Soviet Union. In this way it is somewhat like a combination of the United States Federal Bureau of Investigation (FBI) and the Central Intelligence Agency (CIA). The FBI investigates violations of federal laws within the United States. The CIA conducts intelligence operations to protect the national security of the United States from foreign countries. The KGB combines these functions for Russia along with political and propagandistic activity both inside and outside the Soviet Union.

The GRU is the Russian army's intelligence service. Officially, it is known as the Chief Intelligence Directorate of the Soviet General Staff (*Glavnoye Razvedyvatelnoye Upravleniye*). Technically, the GRU and KGB are separate organizations; actually, they work together, with the GRU serving as an arm of the KGB. Members of each organization refer to members of the other organization as "neighbors" (*sosedi*).

There are members of the KGB and GRU in every Russian embassy throughout the world. The Soviet Union is not, of course, alone in this practice. The United States, for example, also has CIA agents in all its foreign embassies, using diplomatic jobs as a "cover" for their spy roles. But the *number* of Russian spies hiding behind the cover of diplomatic immunity is far greater than that of any other country. One former Soviet spy, Oleg Penkovskiy, has said that 60 percent of all embassy personnel are intelligence officers, either members of the KGB or GRU. Other estimates run even higher. Penkovskiy also reported that from time to time other diplomats within a Soviet embassy are also called upon for espionage work. Some foreign ambassadors have even been KGB members.

By contrast, CIA agents number only a small handful among the far more numerous legitimate staff members of the various U. S. embassies. When the United States embassy in Tehran, Iran, was occupied by Iranian revolutionaries during 1979 and 1980, for example, the Iranians only leveled spy charges against several of the more than fifty embassy staff members. And these charges were never confirmed.

The presence of the United Nations in New York presents the Soviet Union with a golden opportunity to infiltrate KGB and GRU spies into the United States. The opportunity is also unique. Since there is no similar multinational organization physically located in the Soviet Union, neither the United States nor any other free world nation has an equal chance to infiltrate large numbers of spies into Russia. Russia has always taken full advantage of this one-sided opportunity.

Red Agents on UN Payroll

Up until 1972, the United States paid almost a third of the cost of running the United Nations. Since then, it has paid about 25 percent of the overall UN budget, or about $180 million annually. (Russia pays less than half this amount, or about $80 million annually.) Since all of the KGB and GRU agents assigned to the United Nations are officially diplomats, they are on the UN payroll. This means the United States pays at least a quarter of their salaries.

The number of Russian spies estimated to have
been in the United Nations is in the hundreds.
And their official roles have ranged from minor
diplomats all the way up to that of personal aide to
the secretary-general himself.

Arkady Shevchenko, the former UN diplomat
who said that the Killenworth estate was a Soviet
spy nest, knew what he was talking about; he himself had been a member of the KGB. Shevchenko
said that there were also microwave antennas on
one of the UN buildings as well as elsewhere in
New York City. These were used for electronic
surveillance of industry and to intercept vital
U. S. communications.

When Shevchenko defected to the United
States in the late 1970s, he said he had had a
number of KGB agents working for him. One of
these men was Valdik Enger who specialized in
stealing secrets from the offices of U. S. officials.
Enger was eventually arrested by the FBI and
admitted not only to his spy activities but also
spoke of widespread espionage within the UN.
Igor Glagoleff, another defector, confirmed Enger's statement.

Shevchenko also pointed out that UN diplomatic cover gave Russian agents a special advantage
for espionage activities outside New York. Their
immunity as diplomats made it possible for them
to move freely throughout the United States.
Soviet diplomats are supposed to file their travel

plans with the U. S. government, but even when they do so they can easily change these plans. One KGB agent, for example, was supposed to be traveling from New York to Chicago. He did so, however, by way of flying on a chartered plane over the Strategic Air Command (SAC) headquarters in Kansas. Little or nothing is ever done about such UN "diplomatic" activities. In the Soviet Union, on the other hand, the movement of U. S. diplomats, whether or not they are agents, is severely restricted.

Undoubtedly the most flagrant abuse of the United Nations as diplomatic cover by Soviet spies took place during the 1960s and early 1970s when U Thant of Burma was UN secretary-general.

U Thant's Aide a Red Agent

For the entire ten years that he was secretary-general, U Thant's personal assistant was a high-ranking member of the KGB. This man was Viktor Mechislavovich Lessiovsky, whom U Thant knew when Lessiovsky was stationed at the Russian embassy in Rangoon, Burma.

Lessiovsky and U Thant were assigned to the United Nations by their respective governments at about the same time. When U Thant was named secretary-general, he selected his longtime Russian friend as his aide. U Thant later insisted that he never knew Lessiovsky was a member of the KGB and that he was never influenced by the Russian in any of his decisions.

Nevertheless, during his decade as U Thant's aide, Lessiovsky was able to keep his KGB bosses in Moscow fully informed on the inner workings of the UN secretariat. He also kept them up-to-date on the personal as well as professional activities of numerous diplomats representing their countries at the UN. How many of these diplomats were on his personal KGB payroll is not known, but the FBI has indicated there were at least several.

Lessiovsky was also a great tourist. He traveled widely throughout the United States, reporting to Moscow the location of military installations, factories manufacturing tanks and aircraft for the U. S. Defense Department, and other valuable information. As a distinguished UN diplomat, Lessiovsky was a popular guest on college and university campuses, where he frequently spoke on Russia's crusade for world peace.

Shortly after the end of U Thant's term as UN secretary-general, it was publicly made known by the FBI that Lessiovsky was a KGB spy as well as a UN diplomat. Following this disclosure, Lessiovsky returned to Russia, where he became a teacher on the faculties of two centers where KGB and GRU agents are trained. These agents are, of course, trained as spies not only to work in the various Soviet foreign embassies, but also to infiltrate the general population of foreign powers. The most promising KGB and GRU students are given postgraduate courses in infiltrating free world military installations and intelligence organizations.

Soviet Schools
for Spies

THE KGB IS a huge organization. Its members are found everywhere in Soviet society. From the cradle to the grave every Russian is under the eagle eye of this vast secret police organization.

Inside the Soviet Union, the KGB includes not only the traditional plainclothes operatives, who are somewhat like city police detectives or FBI agents. It also includes uniformed men and women trained and equipped like an army. The KGB's so-called forces of the interior number some 400,000 men and women. There are also about 400,000 frontier guards and 350,000 civil police or militiamen who are controlled by the KGB.

The several hundred thousand GRU secret police within the Soviet military forces operate separately from the KGB, but are responsible to the KGB. The KGB in turn reports to the top Communist Political Bureau, or Politburo, which governs Russia.

There are perhaps 100,000 KGB and GRU agents operating outside the Soviet Union. The exact figure, which varies widely depending on the world situation, is not known. These agents or spies are called either "legals" or "illegals." Legals are those agents who have a legitimate cover in a foreign country, such as embassy staff members or United Nations diplomats. As such, they have diplomatic immunity. Illegals are agents sent in to live among the general population of a foreign country with no "legitimate" cover other than the cover they themselves create to blend in with the local society. They have no diplomatic immunity and if caught, they are not simply returned to Russia but are subject to prosecution as spies. Such agents are taught to deny any connection with Soviet intelligence organizations if they are apprehended. This, of course, makes it extremely difficult to prosecute them. For this reason, Soviet spies caught operating within the United States are often simply exchanged for American spies caught in the Soviet Union. Even spies who are successfully prosecuted may be exchanged by the two nations.

One of the most famous cases involved the Soviet illegal, Colonel Rudolf Abel, and the American spy plane pilot, Francis Gary Powers. Under various aliases, KGB-agent Abel operated in the United States for several years before he was caught and jailed. Convicted as a Soviet spy, Abel was sentenced to a long jail term. But he was finally released in exchange for CIA-pilot Powers, who was shot down while on a flight over Russia.

The Case of the Alert Newsboy

An incident that occurred to an alert teenaged newsboy in the summer of 1953 helped unmask KGB-agent Abel. The boy was James Bozart, thirteen, who was making his regular weekly collection rounds in an apartment building in Brooklyn, New York.

One of his customers gave young Bozart a handful of change. Outside on the sidewalk, the boy accidentally dropped the coins. When he picked them up, he was startled to discover that one of the nickels had split open and inside was a tiny piece of photographic film.

Jim Bozart was a bright boy who liked to read. Among his favorite books were spy stories. Consequently, he knew exactly what he was holding in his hand. It was a piece of microfilm, a page of writing photographically reduced to miniature size so it could easily be concealed—as it *was* concealed in the broken nickel.

Young Bozart also collected coins. For a few moments he was tempted to keep the coin and its contents as an oddity to add to his coin collection. But he knew that enemy agents used microfilm to pass secret messages back and forth. He also knew what he must do. Jim Bozart, somewhat reluctantly, turned the broken nickel and the piece of microfilm over to the local police.

The Brooklyn police in turn forwarded the microfilm to the FBI. The FBI enlarged it, and Jim Bozart was eventually proved to be right. It was a message in code to a Russian agent who had recently arrived in the United States. This agent was not Colonel Abel but another illegal, Reino Hayhanen, who had been sent from Russia to aid Abel in his espionage activities in the United States.

Abel had been a successful illegal since 1948. He had entered the country through Canada. One of his cover names was Emil Robert Goldfus. His cover activity was that of photoengraver. Secretly, he gathered atomic and military information which he radioed in code to the Soviet Union. Where and how he gathered this and other vital information was never disclosed, even after Abel was arrested, questioned, tried, and convicted. But the volume of information that he gathered was so large that his KGB bosses agreed he should have an assistant. That assistant was KGB-agent Reino Hayhanen.

Hayhanen, however, proved to be a disappointment as an agent. He was a drunk and, worst of all, careless—as was evident in his allowing the concealed microfilm to fall into the hands of newsboy Bozart. Eventually, Hayhanen became such a failure that he feared for his life at the hands of his own espionage service, the KGB. To protect himself, he defected to the United States authorities. This action and information on the microfilm led to the unmasking of Colonel Rudolf Abel, alias Emil Goldfus.

Abel was sentenced to thirty years in prison in November of 1957. He remained in the Atlanta, Georgia, federal penitentiary with no hope of parole until the spring of 1960. On May 1 of that year, Francis Gary Powers was shot down in a high-altitude U-2 spy plane while on a CIA aerial reconnaissance mission photographing missile sites near Sverdlovsk, Russia. Powers escaped unharmed and the special equipment in his plane was undamaged.

Negotiations began immediately between the United States and the Soviet Union to arrange an exchange of the two prisoners, but it was not until February of 1962 that the exchange took place on the Glienicker Bridge in Germany, which runs between Soviet-held East Berlin and the free world's ally, West Berlin. After the exchange, Powers eventually returned to civilian life as a private pilot. Abel became a teacher at a KGB school in Moscow. His subject: how to operate successfully as an illegal in the United States.

In recent spy stories, illegals such as Colonel Abel frequently have been called "moles." This term is believed to have been invented by the writer John Le Carré and has since been adopted by most of the world's intelligence services. It was not originally an intelligence tradecraft term, however.

Recruiting New Agents

The enormous size of the army of Soviet secret police on duty both inside and outside Russia makes the constant recruitment of new members a necessity. Recruitment for the GRU in the military services is not especially difficult. In every army or air force barracks and in every ship's wardroom in the navy there are several members of the GRU. Thus, the entire military establishment is honeycombed with Communist spies reporting on their own comrades. These military moles not only keep their superiors informed about the morale and loyalty of their comrades but also report the names of possible GRU recruits.

These prospects are then interviewed by their superior officers. If they express an interest in intelligence work—most do, since the improvement in the standard of living for GRU agents is legendary — a thorough check is made of their background. If they pass this test and are approved by the KGB—no one can be appointed to military intelligence without KGB clearance— they are immediately sent to service intelligence schools and then on to one of the more advanced spy schools, such as Moscow's Military Diplomatic Academy. Here they study the English language for several years, methods of sabotage and how to prevent it, recruitment of new agents, codes and ciphers, shortwave radio operation and repair, and foreign military organizations. Supervisors at the Military Diplomatic Academy are KGB officers.

There is compulsory military conscription in the Soviet Union. Every male youth, when he reaches the age of eighteen, must undergo from two to five years of military training. Those who do not reenlist are placed in a permanent military reserve. Conscientious objectors are subject to criminal prosecution. The services thus get an opportunity to pick and choose among a fairly good cross-section of Soviet youths as possible GRU candidates. Most draftees, however, are peasant youths without much formal education or training. Many rural children fail to complete the so-called compulsory first eight grades of school. The prime candidates, those young men with good education and training, are gobbled up by the KGB.

Some privileged youths avoid military service entirely by joining the KGB at an early age. Others may go to officer candidate schools, join the military services as officers, and then enter KGB schools. Officers are required to serve for twenty-five years in the military, but some officers cut short their military careers by joining the KGB soon after they are commissioned.

Other KGB members are recruited from the general population either before or after they complete their military training. This includes a few women, but women are a minority in the KGB, as they are in all important professions in Soviet society. Still other KGB prospects are recruited from among foreign populations. These recruits, however, seldom attend spy schools in Russia but work in their native countries under KGB spy masters or case officers.

To become a member of the KGB in the Soviet Union one must have a sterling record. A typical young KGB recruit is what would be called in the United States an "all-American boy." It is not essential that one be a member of the Communist party, but it helps. (Only about 5 percent of the Soviet Union's more than 260 million people do belong to the Communist party, which rules the country.) But if a prospect is not a Communist party member, he or she must prove his or her sympathy and loyalty to the Communist cause.

Russian Youth Organizations

It is essential, however, that the all-Russian-type candidate be or have been a member of the two Communist youth organizations, the Pioneers and the Komsomol.

The Pioneers are roughly similar to the Boy Scouts but with strong political overtones. Actually, they more closely resemble the Hitler *Jugend* or Hitler Youth Organization in Germany before and during World War II. Children between the ages of ten and fifteen are eligible to join the Pioneers, and almost all school children belong. Members wear bright red neckerchiefs with their school uniforms. Through their leaders they are constantly fed Communist propaganda and indoctrinated in the political organization of the Soviet Union.

When children outgrow the Pioneers, they may join the Komsomol, which is an arm of the Communist party. Young people between the ages of fifteen and twenty-seven are eligible. The Komsomol's main task is to educate Soviet youths in communism. Many older Komsomol members are leaders in the Pioneers. Members wear Komsomol badges but no uniforms.

A *Komsomol Hero*

One of the great Komsomol heroes is Pavlik Morozov, a teenage boy who betrayed his own father. During the late 1920s and early 1930s the newly formed Communist government of Russia took over all of the nation's privately owned farms. The government then planned to run these farms on a cooperative basis with their produce being turned over to the central government. No one was to make any profit from agriculture, but all workers were to share in the harvest. This process was called "collectivization."

Collectivization resulted in driving some ten million prosperous peasants, called *kulaks,* from their farms. These dispossessed kulaks were either killed, put in prison camps, or driven out of the country by the secret police.

Pavlik Morozov lived with his family in the rural village of Gerasimovka. His father was a loyal Communist. Nevertheless, when some kulaks from a neighboring farm tried to escape from a secret police raiding party, the elder Morozov hid them in one of his sheds. His son, Pavlik, had been thoroughly taught by his Communist schoolteacher that such acts were disloyal to the nation. As a result, Pavlik reported his father's act to the local authorities and the elder Morozov was executed by a firing squad. A short time later angry peasants hanged the fourteen-year-old Pavlik.

Pavlik Morozov died in 1932. Soon afterward, he was praised as a martyr by the Communists. Today, the home where he betrayed his own father has been made into a national shrine, and several statues have been erected in Pavlik's honor. Both Pioneer and Komsomol youths are taught that Pavlik's deed was that of a young hero of the Soviet Union and that they should pattern their lives after his.

Red Agents Are Well Educated

A potential KGB member must also have a good education. After completing ten years of primary–secondary schooling, Soviet youths are eligible to take college or university entrance examinations. These examinations are difficult and only the best students pass them. Those who do pass may attend any of several dozen excellent schools. College and university students are given a living allowance by the government and are paid bonuses for good grades. The institution most sought after by prospective KGB members, as well as by youths who simply want to become foreign diplomats, is the Institute of International Relations in Moscow. Its rough equivalent in the United States would be Georgetown University, where many future members of the U. S. State Department are trained.

Competition to enter the Institute of International Relations is fierce. Only six hundred new students are admitted each year, and there are usually as many as ten thousand applicants. Most of those admitted are members of privileged families. Theoretically, the Soviet Union is a classless society; actually, there is a great privileged upper class made up of members of the government bureaucracy, the people who rule and administer the Soviet Union. These people get the best food, housing, automobiles, clothing, and other available merchandise. They shop in their own exclusive stores. They make the most money and their children attend the best schools. These privileged few were called the "New Class" by a Yugoslavian critic of communism, Milovan Djilas, and the term has stuck.

At the institute, students study a wide variety of foreign languages, government, history, and Communist party doctrine, and take part in world affairs seminars that may include foreign students. Institute members have a considerable amount of free time despite the stiff course of study, and most of this free time is spent in living the good life of the privileged New Class in the Soviet capital—drinking, eating, and partying.

There are numerous KGB members on the institute faculty who spot potential KGB members among the first-year students. These recruits are required to sign a KGB secrecy oath. Then they take a separate course of study in intelligence methods similar to that followed in GRU schools. Upon graduation they may be assigned to on-the-job training at KGB headquarters in Moscow, or they may be sent to serve apprenticeships in Soviet embassies in foreign countries bordering the Soviet Union.

KGB candidates who do not attend the Institute of International Relations are sent to special KGB training schools. A typical one is located at Novosibirsk in Siberia. It is housed in a four-story building on the town's main street, Krasny Prospekt. Here the discipline is strict, the course of study is demanding, and there is little time for outside partying. The students do manage to find time, however, for heavy vodka-drinking sessions in their dormitory rooms.

Adjoining rooms include lecture halls, laboratories, a library, a gymnasium, and a mess hall. The food here does not meet New Class restaurant standards, but it is far better than that served in military mess halls. Students are trained in counterintelligence techniques (detecting and frustrating foreign intelligence efforts), recruitment of new agents, secret police methods, crowd control, weaponry, criminal law, espionage techniques (the use of codes and ciphers and how to infiltrate foreign installations and agencies), and radio operation and repair.

Within recent years, the study of computers and microelectronics has been added to the KGB curriculum. This is because the United States and Great Britain have had great success in this field, and the Russians have fallen behind. Consequently, both the KGB and GRU have concentrated their efforts on stealing high-technology information as well as equipment from the Western world. Such information and equipment is essential to nuclear guidance systems as well as to satellite communications.

One of the main courses of study at Novosibirsk, as well as at all Soviet spy schools, is the history of the KGB and GRU. By studying the methods of the early Russian secret police organizations, it is felt that today's fledgling Soviet spies will do a better job of learning their own intelligence tradecraft. Likewise, any young person outside Russia who is interested in today's Russian espionage must know something of its history. This is discussed in the next chapter.

IV

The Sword
and Shield of
the Communist Party

THE KGB AND its spy service "neighbor," the GRU, proudly call themselves the "Sword and Shield" of the Communist party of the Soviet Union. But their history predates the formation of the Union of Soviet Socialist Republics (U. S. S. R.) after World War I. In fact, it goes back several centuries to the days of the Russian czars.

The secret police organization of the czars was called the *Okhrana*. It was used mainly to prevent the millions of poor Russian serfs or peasants from organizing a revolution against their royal masters. Members of the Okhrana were notoriously cruel, brutal, and responsible to no one except the czars' personal aides for whatever actions they chose to take against the peasants and other revolutionaries. But the Okhrana was efficient. It kept down numerous potential revolutions or destroyed them shortly after they were born by the simple process of jailing or killing anyone and everyone even remotely involved in revolutionary activity.

Nevertheless, there were those who risked their lives by carrying on underground warfare against the Okhrana. This guerrilla warfare blossomed into widescale peasant revolts in the mid-nineteenth century, which resulted in the partial freeing or emancipation of some forty million serfs in 1861. They still suffered great economic hardships, however. And, as so often has happened in Russia, this freedom was short-lived. Soon it was again replaced by tyranny. It was not until early in the twentieth century that the czarist regime was permanently overthrown—only to be replaced, of course, by an even worse tyranny which continues to the present day.

In 1917, near the end of World War I, there were riots in Petrograd (now Leningrad) protesting the food shortages. Soon, they became a political protest against the country's continued participation in the war. These riots led to a revolution which not only took Russia out of the war but also toppled the czarist regime. Control of Russia was then seized by a group known as *Bolsheviks,* which means "majority men."

The Bolsheviks believed in the extreme left-wing Socialist or Communist teachings of a radical nineteenth-century German philosopher named Karl Marx. The Bolsheviks' goal was the complete overthrow of Russia's social and economic system. Russia's new government would then theoretically be run by the people, or "a dictatorship of the proletariat," as the Communists called it. This actually meant the complete control of the nation's economy and way of life not by individuals but by the state. The "state," of course, would in turn be controlled by a handful of dictators in the Communist Politburo, as it is today.

Lenin's Secret Police

Vladimir Lenin was the leader of the Bolsheviks. One of Lenin's first acts after the Bolsheviks seized power was to establish his own secret police organization. He did this because there were still many people throughout the country who remained loyal to the overthrown Russian government and were willing to fight a civil war to reestablish it. These so-called White Russians—as opposed to the Red Bolsheviks, or Communists—included former royalty, rich aristocrats, prosperous landowners and businessmen, and ex–army and navy officers loyal to the czar.

These "enemies of the people," according to Lenin, had to be sought out and destroyed if the new Communist regime was to succeed.

Lenin's new secret police organization was called the *Cheka,* which stood for "Extraordinary Commission Against Counterrevolution and Sabotage." The first chief of the Cheka was Felix Dzerzhinsky, who had spent a quarter of a century fighting against the Okhrana. Ironically, Dzerzhinsky himself was not a peasant but a well-born aristocrat who nevertheless opposed the czarist government.

Today, Dzerzhinsky Square in Moscow is named after the first chief of the Cheka, and KGB headquarters, generally known as the Center, is located at number 2 Dzerzhinsky Square. Connected to the Center is the notorious Lubyanka Prison, where hundreds of high-ranking anti-Communist prisoners have been tortured and executed. The trouble was that under the hand of "Iron Felix," as Dzerzhinsky has been called, the Cheka became more brutal and terroristic than the Okhrana had ever been.

Soon after his appointment, Iron Felix announced, "We stand for organized terror. Terror is an absolute necessity during times of revolution. The Cheka is obliged to defend the revolution and conquer the enemy, even if its sword does by chance sometimes fall upon the heads of the innocent."

And terror there was. During the next several years, tens of thousands of White Russians were arbitrarily slaughtered. Perhaps another 150,000 starved to death in concentration-camp-like jails. These numbers were modest compared with those that would be tallied a few years later under Joseph Stalin, but they were a black-enough beginning.

Iron Felix and his Chekists—KGB members still call themselves Chekists today—were so busy putting down real or imaginary counter-revolutionists that they had little time for gathering foreign intelligence. This was undertaken by the newly formed GRU.

Military Intelligence Beginnings

The forerunner of the GRU was founded by Leon Trotsky, another leader of the new Communist government, in 1918. It did not become important, however, until 1920. In the spring of that year Poland, hoping to take advantage of the widespread unrest in Russia, invaded the Russian Ukraine. Lenin immediately ordered a counterattack against Poland itself, but due to faulty military intelligence information from the Cheka the Soviet forces were badly defeated.

Dzerzhinsky reacted to this failure by appointing a new man to head the section of the Cheka responsible for supplying military intelligence to the Russian army. This man was Jan Karlovich Berzin, who proved to be something of an intelligence-gathering genius. He soon had agents established throughout Europe, and not only military but also valuable political information began to flow back to Russia. Berzin's organization was, in fact, so successful that it soon became a separate agency, the GRU, operating within the Soviet army.

Even when the GRU became responsible to the general staff of the army, it did not confine its espionage activities to gathering foreign military intelligence. As the Cheka and its successor agencies expanded their foreign-intelligence gathering, this led to a certain amount of rivalry between the two organizations. This rivalry was encouraged by Joseph Stalin when he later replaced Lenin as the Soviet leader.

The Cheka was formally abolished in 1922. This was done for purely cosmetic purposes; that is, to make the Soviet Union look better in the eyes of the world. By then the Cheka had gained such an international reputation as a terroristic organization that foreign countries were refusing to recognize the new Soviet government. The Soviet Politburo decided to replace the Cheka with the innocent-sounding State Political Directorate, or GPU.

But the GPU was still the Cheka as far as atrocities were concerned. In addition, the GPU expanded its secret police role until it entered every phase of Soviet society. Informant networks were built up to report on the activities of every Russian from birth to death. Such is true of the KGB secret police role within Russia today. From peasant to Politburo member, no person escapes its scrutiny—or wrath.

Daily Life in a Police State

It is hard, if not impossible, for people living in a democracy to really understand what daily life in a police state is like. But just think about it for a moment and imagine that everything you do, every move you make, is under the surveillance of a KGB-like organization.

If you live in an apartment building in a city, one of the apartments will be occupied by an agent of the secret police. He or she will know the daily timetable of activities of you and your family. Any change in the timetable will be reported to the authorities. All visitors to your apartment will also be reported. What you and your family eat and drink will be observed to learn if your mother or father is dealing in the black market. One long-time KGB agent has said that it is possible to write a person's biography just by studying his garbage.

What you and your family talk about at the dinner table might also be reported, since the apartment may be bugged. It will certainly be bugged if anyone in the family is under suspicion or investigation. A member of your own family may even be an undercover agent.

If you live in a house in a suburb or rural town, one of your neighbors may be a secret agent. Again, your comings and goings, your friends, your political beliefs, will be known by that agent. To travel anywhere, even from town to town, you will need to show your "interior passport" to identify who you are and why you are traveling.

At school your teachers will be infiltrated by agents who will report on faculty activities, in and out of school. Some of these teachers themselves will be agents, who will report on you. In sports your soccer coach will probably be a member of a Komsomol-like organization with direct ties to the Communist party and its secret police.

To get a job or to change jobs, which is seldom allowed, you will have to have a "work book." The work book indicates how good a worker you are and is something like a school report card. If your work book shows you have taken too much time off, you may be labeled a "parasite" and assigned to a labor camp.

At work you will again be in the presence of undercover agents—at the neighboring desk or workbench or machine. After work your activities will be noted and reported upon.

If you or members of your family, friends, or neighbors speak out against any aspect of daily

life or the government, arrest and a prison camp
sentence may quickly follow.

If you or members of your family plan to flee
the country to escape such never-ending surveillance, this plan may also become known and you
or they will be arrested. If you do escape, your
family will probably be held hostage by the government until you return and are punished. If you
do not return, they will be sent to a work camp
and become "nonpersons" as far as the government is concerned.

Aside from suicide, there is one common escape from this prisonlike existence. This is
through the use of alcohol. Vodka is the water of
Russian life, and the Soviet Union has one of the
highest alcoholism rates of any country in the
world. This is true even among KGB and GRU
members, who live in a prison of their own since
their ranks are honeycombed with secret agents
reporting on other secret agents.

New Names for the Secret Police

One of the ways Soviet officials have continued
to try and launder the image of the secret police
has been to continue to change its name. This has
never fooled Soviet citizens or foreign governments for very long, but nevertheless the effort
has gone on. It is as if the FBI or the CIA had been
given a dozen different titles since they were es-

tablished. Because the Soviet military establishment is even more of a closed society than civilian life and does not have to present any newly polished image to its members or foreign powers, the GRU has continued to be called the GRU.

The successor to the Cheka, the GPU, had not been so named for very long before it became the OGPU (Unified State Political Directorate). It was the OGPU that Stalin turned loose on the peasants in the drive to collectivize Soviet agriculture, an effort which resulted in millions of deaths. Then, again for cosmetic purposes, Stalin abolished the OGPU and established the GUGB, Chief Directorate for State Security. It worked in collaboration with the NKVD, the People's Commissariat of Internal Affairs. Once again, both organizations soon rivaled the Cheka in nature, zealously slaughtering the Soviet citizenry and terrorizing anti-Communists within and outside the Russian borders. Some of these Stalin purges extended right into the Politburo itself, where even a hint of opposition to Stalin was enough to land high-ranking Soviet bureaucrats in Lubyanka Prison.

An early NKVD chief was known as the "Bloody Dwarf." He was Nikolai Yezhov, who stood only five feet tall. But what he lacked in size he made up for in bloodthirstiness. At Stalin's bidding, the Bloody Dwarf ferreted out all Red Army officers whom Stalin suspected of disloyalty. Between 1937 and 1938, some thirty-five thousand suspect officers were killed, all but destroying the Soviet top military command on the very eve of World War II.

Murder of Beria

The Bloody Dwarf was succeeded by Lavrenti Pavlovich Beria. Beria was one of Stalin's favorite aides, who repaid the Soviet ruler's friendship by plotting his overthrow. Beria went about his plans to replace Stalin and rule Russia himself by first gaining complete control of the whole secret police establishment—the NKVD, the GRU, and several other minor offshoots, the MGB (Ministry for State Security) and KI (Committee of Information). He then took over foreign intelligence operations, the control of several hundred thousand border guards and state militia, all political prisons and their inmates, and the industrial police. Taking over the industrial police enabled Beria to gain control of much of Soviet industry, including several military missile factories.

Beria's plans were aided by Stalin's death in 1953. Beria continued to plot and maneuver, using all of his police powers to prevent any of his rivals from replacing Stalin. But the other members of the Communist Politburo were well aware of what Beria was up to. They also knew that if he came to power their chances of remaining in office were somewhat slim. Led by Nikita Khrushchev, who eventually succeeded Stalin, the Politburo members called Beria to the government offices in Moscow's Kremlin, somewhat as Julius Caesar was summoned to the Roman forum. There, also like Caesar, Beria was fallen upon by assassins and, not stabbed, but strangled to death. The Politburo then announced to the world that Beria had been arrested and shot as a spy who had secretly been working for Western intelligence services, including the CIA!

Following Beria's assassination, owners of the *Great Soviet Encyclopedia* received an interesting communication from the government. They were instructed to take a scissors and cut out the pages containing the biography of Beria in their encyclopedias. These pages were to be replaced with a lengthy new article on the Bering Sea, which was conveniently enclosed with the letter from the government. Later, a similar incident occurred when Stalin was debunked.

This method of rewriting history by changing favorites who have suddenly fallen into disfavor from heroes to "nonpersons" or "unpersons" is not uncommon in the Soviet Union. It is as if American owners of *Compton's* or *World Book* were told by the U. S. government to replace their biographies of a former president or high government official every time a rival political party came to power.

When Khrushchev became Soviet premier, he

and other members of the Politburo organized the Russian secret police in much the form that they have today. The KGB was so named on March 13, 1954. It was given its traditional secret police role within Russia (including guarding the nation's borders), plus all spy operations abroad except for those performed by the GRU. The GRU kept its authority to conduct independent secret operations abroad, but was technically responsible to the KGB. This loose arrangement for the control of foreign espionage has continued to cause some conflict between the two agencies; but generally speaking, the two "neighbors" have worked well together.

The Debunking of Stalin

Soon after he took office, Khrushchev also began a massive "de-Stalinization" campaign. While Khrushchev's purpose in debunking Stalin was recognized as an effort to solidify his own role as the new Soviet leader, Western observers knew enough about Stalin's bloody rule to recognize that much of what Khrushchev was saying was the simple truth. Stalin had indeed been one of the worst mass murderers in world history, rivaling even Adolf Hitler. Estimates of the number of people the Soviet secret police had slaughtered under Stalin's reign of terror ran as high as twenty million, and even this estimate was thought by many to be conservative.

And Stalin's secret police had by no means confined their murderous activities within the borders of Russia. Stalin goaded his agents into tracking down his enemies even when they fled the country and went into hiding in foreign lands. The organization that handled these murders was called the Administration of Special Tasks, referred to by other secret police as the "Department of Wet Affairs" (because of its bloody nature). The most infamous "wet affair" handled by this organization was the murder of Leon Trotsky, original Bolshevik, charter member of the Russian Communist party, and founder of the GRU.

As long as Vladimir Lenin—founder of the Soviet Union—was alive, his able friend and aide, Leon Trotsky, was the second most powerful man in Russia. But when Lenin died in 1924, there was an immediate scramble among Communist party leaders for the top job. In this fight Trotsky lost out to Stalin, another member of the Politburo.

Trotsky remained in the Politburo, but he lost all of his important official positions, including his connection with the GRU and the Red Army, which he had virtually created. He continued to oppose Stalin both politically and personally, but it was a losing battle. Stalin was by far the more cunning and ruthless of the two men, and soon he

began to plot for the removal of Trotsky. With
Lenin no longer on hand to protect him, Trotsky
didn't stand a chance.

On trumped-up charges of disloyalty and sub-
versive activities, Trotsky was banished from the
Soviet Union in 1929. For the next decade he lived
as an exile in Turkey, France, Norway, and finally
Mexico. But exile did not silence Trotsky. He continued to publicly denounce Stalin and attempted
to organize foreign Communists into a movement
against the Soviet ruler.

Murder of Trotsky

Stalin responded by sending some two dozen of
his best secret agents abroad to permanently silence Trotsky. Trotsky, of course, was not unaware that Stalin had put a price on his head. In
Mexico the Russian exile lived in a walled villa
protected by several bodyguards. One of these
bodyguards was an American, Robert S. Harte.
Later, there were rumors that Harte had been recruited as a coconspirator by the Soviet secret
police, but these rumors were never confirmed.

In May of 1940, Stalin's agents made an open
attack on Trotsky's Mexican villa. They scaled the
walls and fired several hundred machine-gun bul-
lets into his bedroom. But Trotsky escaped unharmed. When they withdrew, the Russian agents
took Robert Harte with them, who was later found

murdered. This was done, rumor said, to keep Harte from admitting to his part in the assassination attempt.

There was, however, a known Soviet secret agent among Trotsky's friends (Trotsky did not know he was an agent, of course). This man was Jacques Mornard, alias Ramón Mercader. Mercader was always welcome at the villa, and on August 20, 1940, he entered Trotsky's study and hit him over the head with an ice axe used in skiing. The wound was fatal, and Trotsky died the next day in a Mexico City hospital.

Mercader was sentenced to a special political prison for twenty years, where he served his term in relative comfort. Upon his release in 1960, he left Mexico and settled in Communist-controlled Czechoslovakia. At no time did he suffer from lack of money.

Trotsky's murder was a prime example of Stalin's ruthlessly stubborn singleness of purpose. He again proved this in the case of Richard Sorge, one of the most successful foreign agents who ever worked for Russia. In the end, when a word from Stalin would have saved the captured Sorge's life, Stalin refused to admit he had ever known that Sorge even existed. Today, he is one of the great heroes of the Soviet Union.

V

The Spy
Who Was Left
Out in the Cold

IN 1919, SOON after the founding of
the Soviet Union, Lenin also established what he
called the Third International or *Comintern*. Its
purpose was to spread communism throughout
the world. Within the Comintern were many of
Jan Berzin's first GRU agents. One of these
agents was a German Communist named Richard
Sorge.

Sorge was a tall, handsome, rugged man whom
other men admired and women fell in love with.
Early in his career he cultivated the image of a
hard-drinking newspaperman. Some people

thought he was an American journalist named Johnson. Others thought he was a German journalist named Schmidt. Actually, from the time he was in his mid-twenties Sorge was a top-ranking Soviet spy operating in the Far East.

Sorge was born at Baku, Russia, on October 4, 1895. His father was a German engineer working in Russia, and his mother was a Russian. Interestingly, his grandfather was a close friend of Karl Marx, the German philosopher on whose Socialist teachings the Communist party was founded.

When young Richard Sorge was still a boy, he and his family moved to Germany. Still in his teens when World War I broke out in 1914, the idealistic young Sorge immediately enlisted in the German army to "fight for the Fatherland." Both Sorge's ideals and his body were soon shattered by the grim realities of trench warfare, in which he was wounded several times. One of these wounds would cause him to walk with a limp for the rest of his life.

Disillusioned by Germany's defeat in the war as well as by the government that had led his country into disaster, Sorge became interested in Marxism and communism after he was discharged from the army. He followed news about the revolution in Russia and believed that a similar Communist revolution would soon take place in Germany. When it did not, he decided to journey to the new

Soviet Union and become a member of the Comintern. In Moscow he was immediately enlisted as
a Soviet GRU agent.

After a period of training, Sorge was assigned to
several minor spy missions in Scandinavia. Having completed these missions successfully, he was
given his first major assignment. This was in the
Far East at Shanghai, China. Russia's interest in
the Far East was due to the fact that it feared
being attacked by either China or Japan, especially the latter. Sorge was sent to Shanghai to
report on Chinese-Japanese relations and what, if
any, war preparations both countries were making.

In the 1930s, Japan occupied Manchuria, and
Joseph Stalin, who by then was the Soviet ruler,
needed to know if Tokyo's next move would be
against Russia. What was needed was someone to
set up a Soviet spy network right in the Japanese
capital. Sorge seemed to be the logical person for
this job. Acting under his cover as a foreign journalist, Sorge had sent numerous and valuable intelligence reports back to Moscow from Shanghai.
Using the same cover, he was assigned to the
Japanese post.

Sorge in Japan

In Japan Sorge gradually set up his network
with the following personnel:

- Max Klausen, radio operator. Like Sorge, Klausen was a German who had joined the GRU. The two had worked together in Shanghai. His cover would be that of a German businessman.

- Branko de Voukelitch, a Yugoslav who had become a member of the Comintern by joining the Communist party in France. His cover, like Sorge's, would be that of a journalist and photographer. His real role would be to ferret out secret political and military information.

- Miyagi Yotsoku, translator and encoder of messages to be radioed to Moscow. Aside from Sorge, Miyagi was perhaps the most interesting of the group. First of all, he was an American Communist. Born on Okinawa, Miyagi had immigrated to California with his parents, where he had become a promising young artist. He had also come to hate the capitalistic form of government, and especially American capitalists, for their treatment of the Japanese. Marxism and communism, with its philosophy of "equality for all" no matter what one's race, creed, or color, appealed strongly to him. He joined the Communist party in 1931. The next year he was approached by Comintern GRU agents and enlisted to return to Japan and join Sorge's spy ring. He would operate under cover of being a traveling artist returned to his homeland to paint pictures of the countryside.

Each of these members of the Sorge spy ring arrived in Japan separately so as not to arouse suspicion. Miyagi was the last to arrive, in October of 1932.

Sorge took his time about contacting each of his fellow spies. First he allowed them to establish their own cover and make friends. Then, after several months, he inserted previously agreed upon ads in a Tokyo daily newspaper. When his agents responded, Sorge set up meetings with each of them separately, usually in public parks. Never during all of the time they worked together did the four agents meet together in a group.

Before the next year was out, Sorge, de Voukelitch, and Miyagi had begun to make friends in important newspaper and political circles. Their specific mission was to find out detailed plans for the expansion and training of Japan's army, navy, and air force—a major undertaking.

Meanwhile, Klausen set about building a high-powered shortwave radio set from parts he bought one at a time in different establishments in the Ginza, Tokyo's main shopping district. Until such a radio could be built, messages would have to be sent by courier through the Soviet embassy in Tokyo—a dangerous procedure since the embassy, like all foreign embassies, was under surveillance by Japanese security police. Finally, however, Klausen had his radio built. It was a masterful piece of work, powerful enough to send and receive to and from Moscow and small enough to fit into a briefcase. Today, such a

miniaturized radio would not be difficult to construct or to smuggle into Japan. But before the
invention of the transistor it was necessary to use
vacuum tubes, so such a radio had never been
made before.

Sorge was the most immediately successful
member of the spy ring. First of all, he became a
friend and drinking companion of Colonel Eugen
Ott, a military attaché at the German embassy.
Through Ott he became acquainted with various
top-ranking Japanese military officers. But the
most important friendship he formed was with
Ozaki Hotsumi, a Japanese newspaperman with
strong leftist leanings.

Young Ozaki was on the staff of the Osaka
Asahi, a popular Japanese daily. His beat was the
government offices in Tokyo, a job similar to that
of a correspondent for a major American daily
newspaper working out of Washington, D.C. As
such, Ozaki was able to obtain valuable information about Japanese political, economic, and military matters. This he fed to his friend Sorge, at
first totally unaware that he was dealing with a
Soviet intelligence officer. When he did learn
Sorge's identity, Ozaki was in too deep to back
out. This was a typical method of KGB and GRU
recruitment. But Ozaki was quite willing to continue his agent's role, because he was a pacifist
and strongly objected to his country's preparations for war. If these plans were made known, he

believed Japan's warlords would be publicly disgraced.

Miyagi also made friends in military circles and had soon put together a network of seven additional agents. De Voukelitch, through various newspaper contacts, joined the inner circle of *Domei*, the main Japanese news agency which was also well informed about supposedly secret military affairs.

All of the information gathered by the Sorge spy ring was coded by Miyagi and radioed to Moscow by Klausen. During the next several years, Moscow intelligence headquarters had a front-row seat at virtually every top-secret government and military command meeting held in Japan.

Approach of World War II

By the late 1930s, there were general signs that World War II was approaching, and Stalin and other Soviet officials became more concerned than ever about a possible Japanese attack on Russia. If this occurred, the Soviet Union, which had been at odds with Germany, would find itself caught between Germany on one side and Japan on the other. When Italy, Germany, and Japan formally joined together to form the Rome/Berlin/Tokyo Axis, Stalin became more nervous than ever about Russia's having to fight a two-front war. After World War II began in September of 1939, Stalin solved a part of this problem—or thought he did—by signing a nonaggression pact with Germany.

But in Japan, Sorge knew that Hitler would not live up to this nonaggression agreement. In fact, Sorge's sources and those of all of his network among German officials in Tokyo reported that Germany already had definite plans to attack Russia.

In mid-May 1941, Sorge had Klausen radio a specific date for the German invasion of Russia. The attack would take place on June 22. Stalin, however, refused to believe this intelligence information. When the attack did take place on precisely the date Sorge had predicted, Stalin apparently was as surprised as some of his front-line officers, who radioed to military command headquarters in Moscow: "We are being fired upon. What shall we do?" Thus did Stalin and the Russian people begin to pay for Stalin's slaughter of most of the officer corps of the army during his purges of the 1930s.

Despite his severe disappointment at Stalin's failure to accept his network's red-alert message, Sorge continued to carry on his espionage efforts in Tokyo. And soon he was able to do Stalin the biggest favor that was done for him all during the war.

When Germany launched its attack eastward, it was generally assumed that its ally Japan would also shortly attack Russia. This would mean the two-front war that Stalin had long dreaded would become a reality. And with Russia already reeling under the German onslaught, the Soviet Union's defeat would become a very real possibility. When Japan began sending heavy troop reinforcements to Korea and Manchuria, an invasion of Russia seemed just a matter of time.

Although Sorge had long been convinced that Japan had planned no such attack on Russia, he needed firm intelligence information to back up his conviction. In August of 1941, Sorge's Japanese agent Ozaki got him that information. Ozaki learned that at a meeting of the Japanese high command in Tokyo, it was agreed that Japan would confine its expansion efforts to southeast Asia, Indochina, and the Dutch East Indies. If Germany won the war, the high command believed, Hitler would allow Japan to keep whatever gains it had made during the war. Therefore, Ozaki reported, the high command had decided that it would not declare war against the Soviet Union, since it was not really necessary for Japan to do so.

Sorge immediately had Klausen radio the "No Attack!" message to Moscow, following it with a detailed explanation. This time Stalin believed his top east Asian spy. Several hundred thousand of the Soviet Union's Far Eastern forces were removed from Russia's Siberian border and rushed

to the defense of Moscow, which was just about to
fall to the German *Wehrmacht*. Had Moscow
fallen, Russia may well have been driven out of
World War II just as it had been driven out of
World War I. At the very least, Sorge's message
and Stalin's order to shift troops to the defense of
the Soviet capital played a major role in the ulti-
mate defeat of Hilter's Germany.

For the next several months, Sorge and his ring
turned their efforts toward trying to find out just
what Japan's plans were regarding the United
States. Negotiations were going on between the
two countries that could lead to continued peace.
If they broke down, as Sorge suspected they
would, there would be war.

But Sorge's efforts in this area were hampered
by the fact that he and his agents were suddenly
aware of the fact that the Japanese suspected
them of being spies. One of Sorge's girlfriends, of
which he had several, was picked up by security
police and questioned. When she was released,
she reported to Sorge that he was under suspicion.

Sorge's Cover Is Broken

The Japanese had known for months that there
was such a spy ring in operation, because they had
picked up several of Klausen's radio transmis-
sions. But they had been unable to break the ring's
code, and they had been unable to track down

Klausen because he moved quickly after each transmission, carrying his radio-laden briefcase with him.

The Japanese had always kept as close a watch on foreigners entering Japan as the Russians had on foreigners in the Soviet Union. But now Sorge and his ring were aware of an even closer surveillance. In the fall of 1941, Sorge learned of Japan's definite plans to attack Pearl Harbor before the year was out. But before he could transmit the information, tragedy struck the Sorge spy network.

Early in October, Miyagi was arrested by Japanese security police. A former California friend of his had recently visited Japan. This friend was known to be a Communist and suspected of recruiting Japanese to join the Comintern. He was interrogated by intelligence officials. During the interrogation he mentioned he was a friend of Miyagi. Up to that time, neither the Japanese intelligence organization nor the police had been in the least suspicious of Miyagi. They were now.

Miyagi was brutally interrogated after his arrest. The fact that he was a native Japanese and suspected of being a traitor to his own country made his interrogators especially angry. Although he tried to commit suicide to avoid confessing, his suicide attempt was frustrated and the brutal questioning continued. Finally, Miyagi confessed and named Sorge, de Voukelitch, Klausen, and Ozaki as his coconspirators. All were quickly arrested, and in searching their apartments the police found ample evidence of espionage to convict them with or without confessions.

Richard Sorge and Ozaki Hotsumi were given death sentences. Max Klausen and Branko de Voukelitch were sentenced to life imprisonment. Before he could be sentenced, Miyagi Yotsoku died in prison from the effects of his interrogations. All of the Japanese agents recruited by the Sorge ring were also given stiff prison sentences.

Stalin Abandons Sorge

Sorge was convinced that somehow he would be rescued by his Soviet spy masters. All during the months and years of preparation for the trial, the trial itself, and the numerous appeals that carried the case to the emperor of Japan himself, Sorge waited for and believed in Soviet intervention. What he thought would happen, according to his statements to various newspaper people who were allowed to interview him, was that he would be exchanged for one or more top Japanese spies being held by the Soviet government. But then he learned that just such an effort had been made by the Japanese government—it was another reason for the long delay in carrying out his sentence—to Premier Joseph Stalin, and Stalin had refused to discuss the matter or even to admit he knew of Sorge's existence.

Sorge and Ozaki were executed on November 7, 1944. For the next twenty years the Soviet government continued to treat Sorge as a nonperson. Then suddenly someone in the Kremlin decided that Sorge should be "rehabilitated." Long stories about his feats in helping to save Russia during World War II began to appear in *Pravda* and other Soviet newspapers. He was awarded one of the nation's highest honors, Hero of the Soviet Union. A street and a merchant ship were named after him. Even a postage stamp commemorating him was issued. All of which could do very little good for the dead and too-long-forgotten spy, whom his Soviet masters for almost a quarter of a century had left out in the cold.

VI

The Illegal

SHORTLY AFTER THE END of World War II, there drifted onto a farm near Minot, North Dakota, a young man looking for work. It was wheat harvesting time, so the youth had no trouble getting a job. He was a hard worker, and when the harvest was over he was asked to stay on as a regular hired hand.

This young man had an interesting story. His name, he said, was Nicholas De Groot. He claimed to be a Canadian citizen with a renewable work permit which allowed him to stay on for extended periods in the United States. Nevertheless, from time to time he returned to Canada for a few days, supposedly to report to Canadian immigration officials. He also claimed to be in his late teens, and his papers, if anybody cared to look at them, confirmed this fact.

Nick De Groot was pretty much a loner, keeping to himself except for occasional Saturday-night trips into the local town of Hanford. On these Saturday-night excursions he usually did nothing more than have two or three bottles of Grain Belt beer at Franey's Pool Hall and shoot a few games of snooker. He was an excellent snooker player, it was later reported. After his second or third bottle of beer, young Nick De Groot sometimes loosened up a bit, and gradually his pool parlor cronies came to know a bit more about him.

Tall, blond, and good-looking Nick De Groot could easily have passed for a Swede, of whom there were many in this part of North Dakota. Actually, Nick said, he was originally from the Russian Ukraine, where his grandparents had settled in the nineteenth century. His grandparents were part of a rather large Dutch group who had migrated from the Netherlands to the Ukraine because of the increased opportunity for successful farming there. This little-known historical fact—that people, and Dutch people at that, had voluntarily moved into Russia and not fled from there—never failed to intrigue Nick's listeners.

The rest of his story was equally fascinating. Nick had still been in Russia during World War II. Too young to be conscripted, he had nevertheless been put into a labor supply battalion where he and other young people were treated like slaves by their Soviet masters. During the German invasion of Russia, Nick said, his entire family had been killed.

Nick Joins the Allies

Toward the end of the war, young Nick decided to escape from Russia. One night he and a young friend simply left their labor battalion encampment and began to walk south and west. Hiding by day and walking only at night, living off vegetable roots which they dug up in the fields or from occasional handouts from local peasants, they eventually made it to the British military lines along the Dniester River east of Rumania.

One of the units that made up this small British force along the Dniester was Canadian. Not as strict as their British comrades, the Canadians merely questioned the two youths briefly and then more or less adopted them as mascots. As the war drew to a close and Soviet armies took over most of Eastern Europe, the Canadian unit was removed to Italy, Nick said. He and his comrade were allowed to tag along.

In Italy, according to Nick's story, things became a bit stickier, especially when their Canadian friends were alerted for shipment home. Already there was a temporary American govern-

ment (AMGOT) office in Rome to aid in restoring
order following the German evacuation. Nick and
his friend applied at AMGOT for permission to
come to Canada or the United States. When this
permission was denied, Nick's friend decided to
remain in Italy, perhaps even return to Russia now
that the war was over. Nick, however, had nothing and nobody to return to and still wanted to flee
Europe. His Canadian friends, he said, solved his
problem by smuggling him aboard their troop
transport in a barracks bag when they sailed for
Canada.

At Halifax, Nova Scotia, Nick had been smuggled off the troop transport the same way he had
been smuggled on. There he managed to get odd
jobs to earn a living. Soon he had saved enough
money to leave Nova Scotia and get a good-
paying job on the Alcan Highway. This fifteen-
hundred-mile highway between Dawson Creek,
British Columbia, and Fairbanks, Alaska, had
originally been built as a route for military
supplies during the war. The stretch across
Canada was officially turned over to Canada in the
spring of 1946, and it was on paving and improving
the Alcan's gravel surface that Nick De Groot got
a job.

After some months as a highway construction
worker, Nick said, he felt secure enough to visit a
government office and ask for official asylum in

Canada and, if possible, to apply for Canadian citizenship. There had been a certain amount of bureaucratic delay in granting his requests. During this time, Nick said, he had to submit to numerous interviews by government officials, but there was little information he could supply them beyond the rough details of his curious story.

He then had no identity papers, of course, since he had escaped from Europe with nothing more than the clothes on his back. He had no relatives, as far as he knew, remaining in Russia, and the local government in the area he came from was in a complete state of chaos caused by the war. He only remembered a few first names of the Canadian soldiers who had befriended him and was uncertain about the name of the troop ship that had brought him to Nova Scotia. The Canadian officials, Nick admitted, were correct in suspecting that he was conveniently forgetting details about his military benefactors so that he would not get them into trouble. But Nick never told any of these vital details to anybody else, either. In the end, the officials apparently shrugged their shoulders and Nicholas De Groot was granted asylum and permitted to take out his first citizenship papers.

When work on the Alcan Highway ran out, Nick became a transient harvest hand, following the giant combines that moved across Canada. It was this work that had eventually led him down into the United States where, he said, he had heard pay and living conditions were better.

That there were numerous flaws in Nick De Groot's romantic story would have been immediately apparent to anyone who examined it closely. But who would want to? It was such an appealing tale and the young man telling it was such an engaging, innocent-sounding and innocent-looking person, that no one was inclined to doubt him. And if the elaborate tale was a false one, why would it have been made up just so Nick De Groot could wind up as a farmhand in Canada and the United States? It was some little time before the answers to this question and others about young Nick De Groot were answered.

Who Was "Nick De Groot"?

The truth of the matter was that Nicholas De Groot's real name was Fyodor Glebovich Fedorovsky, and he was a member of the Soviet secret police organization that was soon to be renamed the KGB. His actual age was not nineteen but twenty-six, and he had been trained to become an "illegal" operating in North America ever since he had been a boy and belonged first to the Pioneers and then the Komsomol, or Young Communists' League.

When Russia entered World War II on the side of the United States and Great Britain, Stalin immediately demanded all of the Allies' intelligence information. He was given most of what he wanted to know, and what he was not given his secret agents obtained. Churchill, for example, did not wholly trust Stalin and did not want him to know that Britain had broken the German military communications code. Stalin obtained this information from Soviet agents who had penetrated British intelligence. Roosevelt trusted "Uncle Joe," as he called him, but nevertheless did not want him to know that the United States was engaged in developing an atomic bomb. Stalin got this information from his spies who had penetrated the Manhattan Project, the name of the American nuclear program.

As soon as he knew that Germany was going to be defeated in the war, Stalin began to make plans to expand his spy network in Great Britain and the United States. He had never regarded the two countries as anything but temporary wartime allies. After the war they would once again become prime targets for the spread of communism and eventual domination by the Soviet Union. One of the youths selected for the expansion of the Soviet network in North America was Fyodor Fedorovsky, alias Nicholas De Groot.

De Groot was trained for his role as an illegal in

a spy school in the Soviet interior, far removed from the wartime devastation of Moscow and Leningrad. A part of the cover story devised for him was true. He had been born and brought up in the Ukraine. There was also a Dutch colony in the Ukraine, which had been settled there much as De Groot said. But his forebears were not a part of it. They were Russian peasants who had migrated to the Ukraine soon after the Bolshevik revolution. De Groot's father and several uncles had taken part in the revolution and become high-ranking Communist party officials. Their sons were loyal to the Communist cause. As such, they attended the best schools, where they had an opportunity to study foreign languages. De Groot became fluent in English and was soon slated for a role with the secret police. He also had a flare for drawing and his ability to sketch in realistic detail was encouraged by his teachers. In addition, he became skilled in assembling and operating shortwave radios.

De Groot, however, had not drifted into the Canadian military lines at war's end looking for asylum. There had, in fact, been no Canadian troops as far east as the Dniester River. He had sailed to Nova Scotia aboard a Russian freighter and begun his career as an illegal there. He had not applied for Canadian citizenship. All of his official papers had been forged in Russia.

The First "Early Warning" Defense Systems

Soon after World War II ended, the Soviet Union and its former American and British allies became involved in what was called the "cold war." The United States and Great Britain did not actually become engaged in military action against Russia, but the cold war conflict was nonetheless intense. To protect themselves from possible aerial attack by Russia via the polar route, the United States and Canada began to construct a series of radar stations along the northern rim of North America. These outposts, called the Distant Early Warning or DEW line, would signal an alarm if enemy planes approached the continent.

South of the DEW line was constructed what was called the Mid-Canada Early Warning line, and along the United States-Canadian border was the so-called Pinetree Warning System. All of these lines were built in the 1950s.

Later, when both Russia and the United States began to build intercontinental ballistics missiles, a Ballistic Missile Early Warning System (BMEWS) was established in Greenland and Alaska. It and the other early warning systems were connected with the North American Air Defense Command (NORAD), whose headquarters were in Colorado. NORAD's job was to order American and Canadian fighter planes and antiballistic missiles into the air to defend against any Russian aerial attack. This was accomplished by SAGE (semiautomatic ground environment), an electronic guidance system that aided aircraft and missiles in identifying and intercepting enemy planes and missiles.

The Soviet spy who was in on the ground floor to report back to Russia the details about the construction of the first of these early warning systems was young Nick De Groot, the hardworking harvest hand.

The first early warning lines were built rapidly, and just as rapidly Russian intelligence began to learn about them in detail. There were several hundred radar stations, and De Groot pinpointed the sites of most of them. He also provided his Soviet spy masters with detailed sketches of several of the sites, which were all constructed on the same pattern. Once the Russians knew where these early warning stations were and how they were constructed, its air force could make plans to knock them out, or sabotage them from the ground. This would clear the way for an all-out bombing attack on the whole of North America.

De Groot first learned that radar installations were being built along the United States-Canadian border from other farm workers. Several of them, in fact, had gotten jobs on the sites. De Groot quit his job on the farm near Minot and also went to work as a civilian employee at one of the sites. It was not difficult to do. His papers were all in order, and he was a conscientious worker, as his previous bosses were willing to attest.

When he first went to work for the U. S. Army Corps of Engineers, he was employed on sites near Minot. Consequently, he still showed up frequently at Franey's Pool Hall in the village of Hanford. He was not so much of a loner now, and he had an abundant amount of money to throw around. Construction workers' pay was known to be good, of course, but even some of his coworkers were surprised at their friend Nick's seemingly endless supply of it. He was generous about buying them all drinks, especially workers who had been employed on other radar sites elsewhere in the various early warning systems. His curiosity about these other sites also seemed endless, especially their location and whether their construction and defense systems varied.

Nick's Collaborators

At the pool hall, two of the people De Groot became most friendly with were Alex Gregorsky and his son, Peter. They were farmers who had originally come from Russia and settled in the area before the war. De Groot had met them earlier when he had first come into Franey's Pool Hall. But back then when he was still a newcomer and very much a loner, De Groot had been no friendlier with them than with anyone else. This had surprised some people, since De Groot and the Gregorskys were originally Russians and might have been expected to be friendlier with one another. Now, however, the three became all but inseparable, not only on Saturday nights at the pool hall but also on other weeknights, when De Groot frequently visited the Gregorsky farm.

When work on the sites near Minot ended, De Groot learned there was similar work to be had on the Mid-Canada Early Warning line. He journeyed farther north and went to work there. With him went young Peter Gregorsky, who had told his cronies at Franey's before he left that if his pal Nick De Groot could make so much money as a construction worker, so could he. But Peter Gregorsky was not a Canadian citizen and was refused work in Canada. Nevertheless, he hung around the site where Nick was employed for several days until the construction foreman asked him to leave. For security reasons, only employees were allowed in the construction area.

Young Gregorsky returned to the family farm near Minot. But he frequently visited his friend De Groot in a town in Canada where the construction workers gathered in their free time, and De Groot occasionally returned to the Gregorsky farm for short stays.

While working on the mid-Canada project, De Groot expressed great interest among his fellow workers about the DEW line being built in the far north. He had no trouble learning that the DEW line, which was only partially completed, would be made up of some sixty-four radar sites and would stretch some 4,500 miles across Canada from the Aleutian Islands to Iceland.

How could he get a job working on that project in the far north? Nick wanted to know. The reason for his interest, he told his coworkers, was the chance to make even more money than he was making working on the mid-Canada line.

At this point, De Groot ran into his first roadblock. The construction foreman told De Groot that to get work on the DEW line he would first have to be cleared by a department of the Royal Canadian Mounted Police in Edmonton. The foreman also seemed unconvinced by De Groot's reason for wanting to leave his present high-paying job. In addition, the foreman had for some weeks been aware of De Groot's sketching activities in his leisure time. When the foreman asked to see the sketches, they proved to be drawings of De Groot's coworkers, but always in the background were detailed drawings of the radar equipment and antiaircraft gun emplacements. The foreman also recalled De Groot's friend with the Russian-sounding name, who had so reluctantly left the earlier site on which they had been working when he had been refused a job.

Nevertheless, when De Groot showed up at the

foreman's construction shack a few days later and
said he would like a few days off so he could go
into Edmonton and be interviewed by the RCMP,
the foreman agreed to radio ahead to arrange the
interview. He did not, of course, tell De Groot
that included in the radio message would be a
suggestion that the RCMP carefully investigate De
Groot's background and his reasons for suggesting
such a check.

De Groot journeyed to Edmonton in the construction company's airplane. This was a light aircraft which made a weekly mail delivery flight to
the site. When De Groot arrived at the RCMP
headquarters, he was almost immediately ushered
into a large waiting room. He was alone for a quarter of an hour in the waiting room and must have
been surprised to find enclosed in a large glass
case a map of the DEW line with each radar station clearly indicated. He should also have been
suspicious. Perhaps he was. Nevertheless, he
studied the map carefully and was still poring
over it when his interviewer entered the room.

The interviewer was in civilian clothes. He was
warm, friendly, but nevertheless wanted to know
about De Groot's background in some detail. He
was originally Russian, was he not? How did he
get into Canada? Did he have a passport, citizenship papers, any other identification?

The interviewer looked at De Groot's papers,
left the room with them for a few moments, and

then returned to listen to the rest of De Groot's tale. Did he recall the name of the troop ship on which he had arrived in Nova Scotia? Any names of his Canadian army benefactors? Was he certain he had first contacted a Canadian infantry unit along the Dniester?

The interviewer surprised De Groot by asking him the name of his American friend who had also tried to get a job on the mid-Canada line. He, too, was originally Russian, was he not? Where was his family farm located?

By now De Groot was beginning to show obvious signs of suspicion. But his interviewer reassured him. All prospective workers on the DEW line had to undergo similar interrogation. And De Groot would have to admit his story was an unusual one, wouldn't he?

Then the interview was over. De Groot was told to return to his job and it would probably be only a few days before he received clearance for work in the far north. With obvious relief De Groot rose and left.

The Mounties Miss Their Man

But De Groot did not return to his job. In fact, he did not return to the local airfield that afternoon, where he had made special arrangements with the regular pilot to fly him back to the construction site. De Groot had even paid in advance for the extra trip. Unfortunately, no one had been assigned by the RCMP to follow De Groot when he left their office. And when he failed to show up at the airport, the puddle-jumper plane pilot waited an extra two hours and then returned home. Construction workers were notoriously unreliable, the pilot later testified. He assumed De Groot had probably just gone off somewhere and gotten drunk.

It was not until a week later that the foreman at the radar site learned from the pilot making his regular mail delivery flight that De Groot had never appeared for his return flight. The foreman, too, had assumed that De Groot was simply off on a typical construction worker's binge. Now, however, he radioed to Edmonton to report De Groot's disappearance. The RCMP immediately issued a nationwide alert for De Groot's arrest. By then, of course, it was too late. De Groot had disappeared for good.

Meanwhile, however, shortly after De Groot's interview in the RCMP offices, photocopies of his official papers had been turned over to other government offices. The day after De Groot's disappearance became known, the RCMP had a report back that the papers were probably false, since no record existed of De Groot in the immigration offices or elsewhere. De Groot's interviewer was more than relieved, he later reported, that the

DEW line map he had put on such obvious display in his office had been a doctored one that was completely inaccurate in its site locations. The RCMP now wasted no time in notifying the FBI in Washington about De Groot's Russian friends near Minot. The FBI immediately sent a pair of agents to the farm, but it was several days before they discovered a powerful, long-range radio hidden under the floor of one of the farm's outbuildings. The Gregorskys were arrested, and in their first interrogation admitted that De Groot had telephoned them from Edmonton telling them he was under suspicion and that they should destroy the radio. They had thought it too valuable, however, and had decided simply to hide it.

"Nick" Surfaces in Russia

That he did return to Russia is known, because on different occasions when several members of the KGB later defected to the United States, they reported De Groot/Federovsky was a celebrated figure in KGB circles. He had also been put in charge of setting up a true-to-life Canadian village at a special KGB camp at Vinnitsa in the Ukraine. There, an exact replica of a small Canadian town was created, where Russian spies were—and still are—trained for their future roles as illegals in Canada. Right next to it is an equally realistic

American town for prospective illegals to be trained for undercover work in the United States. De Groot also has a supervisory role in the training program at this Hollywood-like stage set, which is authentic right down to stores, telephone booths, mailboxes, a small hotel, bars, restaurants, and American-style buses and taxis. The two towns even have Westernized names. The pseudoCanadian village is called Clifton, and the American town is called Roswell.

Soon after De Groot escaped to Russia, the United States and the Soviet Union were successful in orbiting various vehicles in outer space. When the first Russian orbit was successful, the United States established SPASUR, which stands for the Space Surveillance of objects in earth orbit. Put on guard by De Groot's earlier success in obtaining information about the several early warning lines, the United States at first successfully thwarted numerous KGB and GRU efforts to obtain information about SPASUR. But gradually even some of these secrets began to leak out. With the growth of computerized electronic surveillance devices, the Western world has had increased difficulty thwarting Russian espionage efforts. And so this never-ending fight for maintaining national security goes on and on and becomes more and more sophisticated each year.

The Gregorskys, it was learned after a lengthy

interrogation, were not true illegals in the sense that they had been trained in Russia to operate as spies in the United States. They were, however, in the United States illegally. Their passports and immigration papers were counterfeit. The Gregorskys had been well-to-do landowners—*kulaks*—in Russia who had fled to escape murder at the hands of Stalin's secret police. They had paid a small fortune for the counterfeit documents and to be smuggled out of Russia. In the United States they had lived quietly as modestly successful farmers—until De Groot had arrived on the scene.

De Groot had evidently learned of their background through his secret police contacts in Russia and had blackmailed them into letting him use their farm as a safe place from which to send his messages to Moscow. It was De Groot who had operated the radio, but Peter Gregorsky had acted as a courier in sending De Groot's sketches to a blind post office box in New York City. The radio had been sent to them by another of De Groot's sources in the east. It had arrived in a packing crate labeled as farm machinery and had been sent by railway express. The FBI attempted to trace this shipment as well as to learn the name of the boxholder in the New York post office, but without success. Fictitious names had been used in both instances.

Despite their relative innocence, the Gregor-skys were quickly brought to trial and sentenced to twenty-five years in a federal penitentiary. When they were released from prison, they returned to farming in Wisconsin under an assumed name.

How De Groot escaped from Canada is not known. It is probable that he had memorized the addresses of certain safe houses in several Canadian cities, but none were ever found in Edmonton. Several such hideaways were later discovered in Montreal, Quebec, and Toronto, and it is possible he somehow made his way to one of them, where he remained until he could be smuggled back to Russia.

VII

The Tunnel

A<small>T THE END</small> of World War II, Germany was divided into occupation zones by the four victorious Allies: the United States, Great Britain, France, and the Soviet Union. They also divided Berlin, prewar capital of Germany, into four such zones. The city was temporarily governed by an Allied Command Council, or *Kommandatura*.

From the beginning, Russia refused to cooperate with the other Allies and soon withdrew from the Kommandatura. It also began to demand that the other Allies get out of Berlin. This they refused to do, despite a Russian attempt to blockade the city and prevent food, fuel, and other supplies from reaching the civilian population. The United

States and Great Britain broke the blockade with
an around-the-clock airlift that operated seven
days a week in all weather. But the Russians continued their warlike attitude toward their former
allies, and Berlin was split into Soviet-controlled
East Berlin and free West Berlin. This division
remains in effect today.

In 1958, at the height of the cold war, Russia
renewed its demands that the whole of Berlin be
declared a demilitarized free city and gave the Allies six months to leave. This ultimatum was ig-
nored, because the Allies recognized it as a Soviet
device to establish its own kind of Communist regime in the part of Berlin that remained free.
Meanwhile, thousands of East Germans and other
refugees continued to pour out of East Berlin into
West Berlin to escape Soviet oppression. Since
the end of the war more than 100,000 East German
refugees a year have fled the Russian zone.

The Berlin Wall

In the summer of 1961, the Russians decided to
put a stop to this exodus by erecting a wall between East and West Berlin. The wall was built of
concrete topped by barbed wire. At regular inter-
vals there were machine-gun emplacements atop
the wall as well as huge searchlights to light up the
area at night. Despite these primitive precautions,
desperate East Germans continued to climb over

the wall and escape to freedom. Many were killed doing so, but many managed to make it.

In addition to this traffic in refugees between East and West Berlin there also developed a major traffic in espionage agents. This was two-way traffic, with as many American and British agents making their way into East Berlin as there were KGB and GRU agents entering West Berlin. Since the whole area was filled with Soviet and Allied troops and military installations, it became important that each side find out as much secret military information as possible about the other. In time, the two Berlins became so thick with agents that gathering intelligence became all but impossible.

Many efforts were made to break this intelligence stalemate, but none were successful. Finally, the United States and Great Britain came up with an ingenious idea: to dig a huge tunnel between West and East Berlin. This tunnel was not planned as a secret passageway for American and British agents to enter the Soviet sector. Instead, it was to lead to points beneath certain key Russian buildings in East Berlin—KGB and GRU headquarters, among others. At these points, the tunnel would be crammed full of sophisticated electronic listening devices, which would pick up and record or transmit directly to Anglo-American intelligence offices in West Berlin all conversations and military telephone traffic in the Soviet zone.

Building the Berlin Tunnel

With the greatest possible secrecy, this Allied espionage tunnel under the city was excavated at a cost of more than $30 million. Its entrance was deep in West Berlin, and the tunnel led for two thousand yards deep into East Berlin. It was about fifteen feet underground, braced with steel supports, and was high enough so that a six-feet-tall man could stand upright in it.

Above the entrance to the tunnel in the American sector was a radar station. Installing the radar station to camouflage the tunnel entrance was the idea of the CIA's chief-of-station in Berlin, William K. Harvey. Harvey also supervised the construction of the tunnel and said afterward his biggest problem was in figuring out ways of secretly hauling away the several thousand tons of dirt dug out from beneath Berlin. The dirt disposal problem was finally solved by ordering major street repairs in the surrounding area and using the road construction crews to load the dirt into their trucks and then haul it away.

One arm of the tunnel was dug to within a few feet of the main telephone cable connecting the Soviet high command in East Berlin with Moscow. Other nearby cables connected the Soviet general staff, Russian embassy, and KGB and GRU headquarters with all of the Russian military units in East Germany. Each of these cables contained numerous telephone lines. In all, there were almost five hundred separate telephone lines readily accessible to American and British intelligence operators once the tunnel was completed. U. S. Army technicians tapped into these Russian telephone lines and set up several hundred tape recorders to monitor and record all diplomatic, military, and intelligence conversations among all of the Russian installations in East Germany and between East Berlin and Moscow.

For almost a year, American and British intelligence had a field day reaping a harvest of secret information from their telephone taps in the Berlin tunnel. Among other things, they learned the Russian order of battle, or the location of every Red military unit in East Germany. Even more valuable was learning the identities of numerous KGB and GRU agents.

Double Agent George Blake

Then the listening post was discovered. Or rather, it was revealed to the Russians—not by any of their intelligence agents in East Berlin, but by a double agent, a member of British Military Intelligence, Department 6 (MI-6), who was actually a Soviet spy.

The double agent's name was George Blake.

George Blake was probably the last man in the

British intelligence service anyone would have suspected of treason. This, of course, was what made him so valuable to the KGB.

Happily married, the father of two young boys, Blake had worked for MI-6 for many years. Although Blake was a British citizen, he was not British by birth. He was born in Holland and christened George Behar.

Young Behar was in his teens when the Germans invaded Holland in 1940 early in World War II. His family escaped to England, but George remained behind to fight against the Germans as a member of the Dutch secret underground army. As a resistance fighter, George had contact with British intelligence agents operating in Europe. One of these agents urged George to go to London, where he could give much valuable information about the Germans to British intelligence and also help train other prospective agents. Reluctantly, George agreed to do so.

In London, George himself underwent further training and was eventually assigned to British Naval Intelligence. An extremely bright young man, George studied foreign languages in his spare time. After the war, he remained in naval intelligence and he and the other members of his family who were in England changed their name to Blake.

During the immediate postwar period, George

Blake was married to an English girl and took his wife with him when he was assigned to Hamburg, Germany, in the office of naval intelligence. By 1948 George's superior officers thought so much of his abilities that they recommended he be sent to Cambridge University in England to study Russian. Actually, he had never had more than the equivalent of a high school education. Before he received a degree at Cambridge, however, he was assigned to the British Foreign Service as an intelligence agent. His first assignment was to the British embassy in Seoul, South Korea. He was on duty there in 1950 when Communist North Korea attacked South Korea. Before the members of the British legation could leave, Seoul was overrun by North Korean troops and George Blake was one of those taken prisoner. Fortunately, his wife and two infant sons had remained behind in England when George had been assigned the Korean post.

A certain amount of mystery still surrounds George Blake's time as a prisoner of the North Koreans. Numerous fellow prisoners later reported that he was a hero, standing up bravely before his captors, refusing to obey their orders, aiding fellow prisoners when they were ill or suffering from beatings by the enemy, even helping to plan and take part in several unsuccessful escape efforts.

Blake Becomes a Red Agent

But George Blake himself later confessed it was in North Korea that he defected from British intelligence and became a double agent for Communist Russia.

The instrument used to convert Blake to the Communist cause was probably a remarkable Soviet agent named Gregory Kuzmitch. Kuzmitch spoke English fluently and had an outstanding record for "turning" both British and American agents into Russian agents. He was sent to prisoner-of-war camps along the Yalu River in North Korea to try and continue his successful conversion efforts there.

At this time there was a great deal of talk and speculation in the world press about the "brainwashing" of captives held by the Communists in North Korean prisoner-of-war camps. A number of these prisoners were Americans. The United States had provided the majority of combat troops when the United Nations had agreed to armed resistance against the North Korean attack. These American troops successfully stemmed the North Koreans and finally drove them out of South Korea. But American casualties were heavy, including thousands who were taken prisoner.

Nobody seemed to know exactly what "brainwashing" consisted of, but its effects were to rid prisoners of their beliefs in and loyalties to their native countries and turn them into Communists. After the war, returning POWs reported that they had been starved, tortured, and then given lectures on communism. Some soldiers apparently accepted the Communist teachings to avoid further torture and mistreatment. But they only remained "brainwashed" until the war ended. Actually, only a handful of Americans and British ever truly gave up their beliefs in a democratic and free way of life to join the Communist cause, but apparently one of those who did was George Blake.

Kuzmitch realized he had a potentially valuable double agent on his hands in George Blake, if he could turn him from the British. Kuzmitch did not resort to torture or other crude methods. This very fact may have influenced Blake. The fact that he was a POW for three years may also have affected his judgment.

Kuzmitch saw to it that Blake was taken off regular POW work details, provided him with extra rations, and then through mental persuasion began to convert him to communism. Kuzmitch was wise in the ways of Western society and spoke to Blake long and frequently about the unfairness of the class system in Great Britain, the downtrodden poor throughout the capitalistic Western world, and the injustice of United Nations forces being in Korea. In the end, George Blake agreed to become a double agent, but he insisted he would not accept any payment from Russia for his spy work.

Ironically, Kuzmitch defected to the United States at the end of the Korean War and was a valuable source to the CIA about the Soviet intelligence system. Kuzmitch always insisted he had little or nothing to do with Blake's becoming a double agent. In fact, he never mentioned Blake's name until years later.

A Hero's Welcome

Blake returned to England as something of a hero when the Korean War armistice was signed in 1953. He was given several months' leave for rest and recuperation and then went to work for British MI-6. He held down a desk job evaluating British agents' reports from the field. Many of these reports, as well as other secret papers, he photographed and turned over to a KGB agent in London.

In 1955, Blake was himself assigned to duty in the field. His post: Berlin. Here he successfully continued his spy work for several years, turning over all manner of intelligence information to Soviet KGB agents in East Berlin. To make sure his British superiors remained satisfied with Blake's work, the Russians provided him with various harmless but apparently valuable Soviet documents that he could give to the British. The most valuable and most damaging information Blake provided the KGB were the names of dozens of agents working for American and British intelligence. The betrayal of these agents in most cases led to their deaths. Some fifty of them were even put on display at a public "show trial" in Moscow before being sentenced.

When the Berlin tunnel was first built, Blake did not know about it. In fact, it was successfully operated for many months before Blake suspected its existence. Information gained from the tunnel's telephone taps was simply turned over to American and British intelligence headquarters with no indication as to its source. This was done, of course, to keep the existence of the tunnel a secret by keeping all information about it on an absolute "need to know" basis.

But Blake was an excellent agent, and soon after intelligence information gained from the tunnel telephone taps began to appear on his MI-6 desk, he became curious as to its source. He became doubly curious when his Russian contacts began to query him about serious intelligence leaks that were occurring in Soviet command headquarters. Discreetly, Blake questioned his British superiors about the source of the excellent Russian intelligence he was receiving. He needed to judge its accuracy, he said, so he could plan his own spy activities. It took Blake almost a year, but finally he was included among the short list of

MI-6 members who "needed to know" about the tunnel.

When Blake was finally let in on the secret, he did not immediately turn this information over to his KGB contact in East Berlin. Instead, he told him he wanted a special "eyes only" report sent to the head of the KGB "disinformation" desk at Karlshorst, East Germany. Through his Soviet contacts, Blake knew that a Disinformation Department had recently been established in Moscow under General Ivan Ivanovich Agayants. Agayants in turn had sent fifteen Soviet disinformation specialists to Germany. It was the job of these specialists to feed false intelligence information to the West, but this information had to appear to be absolutely authentic.

Disinformation Fed to Allies

Blake's shrewd move proved to be as successful for the Russians as the nine months of undiscovered telephone taps had been for the United States and Great Britain. Instead of simply exposing the tunnel for all the world to see, the Soviet KGB specialists at Karlshorst began feeding vast quantities of false information, or "disinformation," into a wide variety of telephone conversations. This the Russians also did on their own "need to know" basis, so they were able to keep secret their awareness of the tunnel and use it for their own purposes for many months.

When CIA and MI-6 agents finally realized that the tunnel was no longer a secret, they abruptly abandoned it, leaving behind all the equipment. Once they decided to move out, they had to move fast so none of their personnel would be captured. Immediately, the Russians went public with their discovery, exposing its presence to journalists from around the world. This exposure proved to be a major propaganda success for the Soviet Union, since it proved that East Berlin residents were the victims of Western espionage. Photographs of the interior of the tunnel with all its electric gear in place were printed in newspapers throughout the world.

George Blake's role in disclosing the existence of the tunnel to the KGB was not immediately discovered by the British. In fact, his successful career as a Russian mole in MI-6 went on for some time. His work in Berlin was so highly regarded by the British that he was allowed to return home for a long vacation. Then he worked for a time in MI-6 headquarters, until he was sent to the Middle East as one of a small group of foreign office students chosen to study at an Arabic university in Lebanon. The foreign office thought that adding Arabic to his knowledge of languages would help Blake become a valuable aide in the troubled Middle East.

Blake's Cover Is Blown

But while Blake was in the Middle East, his past began to catch up with him. In West Berlin, a man named Horst Eitner was arrested as a spy by Allied intelligence. In prison in West Berlin, Eitner named several British intelligence agents who were working as double agents for the KGB. One of those he named was George Blake.

Despite the fact that nobody in MI-6 in Berlin could believe Eitner's accusation against Blake, the report was turned over to British counterintelligence. Counterintelligence investigators, many of whom knew Blake, did not press their search into his past, since they were convinced Eitner was simply accusing everybody in sight to save his own skin.

But then a Communist member of the Polish secret police, a man named Anthony Alster, defected to British intelligence officers in West Germany. In his debriefing by MI-6 officers, Alster also named Blake as one of the most successful double agents the Russians had working for them. Alster even turned over to the British several reports filled with secret British information which had been supplied by Blake.

The rest happened quickly. George Blake was recalled from the Middle East and confronted with the accusations against him. Blake soon made a full confession of all of his activities as a double agent. Shortly afterward, he was brought to trial for having committed offenses against the British Official Secrets Act. He was quickly found guilty and sentenced to forty-two years in prison.

But the saga of George Blake was not yet over. He began to serve his sentence at Wormwood Scrubs Prison in London. He proved to be a model prisoner. In prison he made friends with another inmate, Sean Bourke. Bourke was serving a short term as a member of the Irish Republican Army, a revolutionary organization opposed to British rule in Ireland. Bourke had been found guilty of mailing a bomb to a British police station. Blake and Bourke soon began to make plans to escape.

From the first weeks that Blake was imprisoned, there were constant rumors that the Soviets were going to try and free him. Consequently, an extremely close watch was kept on him. (Apparently, however, his mail was not censored.) This close watch prevented Blake and Bourke from actually putting any escape plans into action. But Bourke was released in 1966, and before he left prison he told Blake he and his IRA friends would help Blake to freedom. Bourke was not successful in enlisting his friends, so he planned the escape himself.

Bourke rented a room in a house near the prison and hired a car. He wrote and told Blake to be near the wall in the prison yard at a certain hour on October 22, 1966. Bourke knew this was the time when prisoners were allowed into the yard for exercise. At that precise time, Bourke wrote, he would throw a rope ladder over the wall and Blake was to climb it. Then he would have to jump from the top of the wall to freedom.

The Escape

The escape went exactly as planned. Bourke drove up in his car at the agreed-upon time, threw the ladder over the wall, and Blake climbed it. In jumping from the wall, Blake was briefly knocked unconscious, but Bourke dragged him into the car and drove to his nearby rooming house. Once they were there, he was able to help the now fully conscious Blake to his room and then Bourke left to dispose of the car in a distant part of the city.

Bourke and Blake lay holed up in their secret room for several days. Then they were contacted by Soviet agents, with whom Blake had kept in touch while he was in prison. These agents smuggled both Bourke and Blake out of London and onto a Soviet freighter. Bourke had agreed to go with Blake to Russia because he knew the British police would learn of his role in helping Blake escape and return him to prison.

But Bourke only remained in Moscow for two years, returning to Ireland in 1968. The British government was unsuccessful in getting Bourke extradited from Ireland and back to England.

In Moscow, Blake was greeted as a hero. Awarded one of the Soviet Union's highest honors, the Order of Lenin, his exploits for Russia were also widely publicized in the Russian press.

Why Blake defected to the KGB has never been fully understood by Western intelligence experts. But he was not the first British agent to do so— nor, unfortunately, would he be the last.

VIII

The Old Boy Spy Network

THERE ARE ALWAYS rumors circulating in intelligence circles that the head of a particular country's intelligence services is actually an enemy spy. Russia's Nikita Khrushchev, for example, tried to take advantage of this kind of rumor when he seized power after Stalin's death and had Lavrenti Beria assassinated. That Beria, Stalin's murderous secret police chief, was actually a spy for Western powers was an almost laughable accusation as far as Western intelligence agencies were concerned. But it gave Khrushchev a good excuse for getting rid of Beria and also enabled him to dismantle Beria's secret police organization and establish the KGB, which would be loyal to Khrushchev.

Not infrequently it has also been rumored that there is actually a Soviet mole at or near the top of America's CIA. These rumors also have so far proved to be, if not laughable, at least unfounded. In Great Britain, journalist and spy specialist Chapman Pincher has claimed that the late Sir Roger Hollis, who long headed MI-5 (British Military Intelligence, Department 5), was actually a KGB agent and the biggest spy of all. This claim, however, has never been confirmed. But there was actually one man who made it almost all the way to the top of the British secret services before he was exposed. As it was, he did become England's anti-KGB intelligence chief, charged with gathering secret information about the very Soviet agency he was working *for*. He also was able to penetrate to the very heart of secret FBI and CIA operations in the United States.

Allen Dulles, former head of the CIA, called this man "the best spy the KGB ever had." His name was Harold A. Philby, known simply as "Kim" Philby. He was truly a master spy for the Russians. Also deeply involved in the Kim Philby case were three other British subjects who were actually Soviet agents. They were Guy Burgess, Donald Maclean, and Anthony Blunt.

Kim Philby was born in India in 1912. He was the son of Harry St. John Philby, a British civil service officer then serving in India, and Dora Philby. The Philbys later returned to England, where young Kim attended a public school. (In Great Britain so-called public schools are actually private.) While he was still in his teens, Kim enrolled at Cambridge University. At Cambridge he became interested in socialism and made his first contacts with members of the Communist movement.

Communism Spreads During the Depression

In order to understand what it was about communism that attracted young people like Kim Philby—and there were many such youths, not only in Europe but also in the United States—it is necessary to understand something about the atmosphere of the times. World War I, which ended in 1918, was followed by a period of booming economic prosperity during the 1920s. Then, in the 1930s, a worldwide economic depression set in. In Great Britain, as elsewhere, millions of people were out of work and not a few were actually starving.

To young people like Philby and his friends, it seemed that there must be something wrong with their countries' governments to allow such conditions to exist. Perhaps a revolution was necessary to overthrow the Western capitalistic governments that had gotten the world into such a mess. But what should they be replaced with? Why not communism? The Russian people had overthrown their government and replaced it with a new system in which all citizens were to share and share alike. There was to be no privileged class or classes in the Soviet Union, as there were in the Western world. Every citizen would be treated equally and every citizen in return would contribute his or her talents and work efforts equally.

This was truly an idealistic picture of a government, and it appealed strongly to the Kim Philbys of the world. What was more, with a model like the Soviet Union to copy, they felt their own governments could be overthrown and one patterned after Russia's established in its place. This meant joining the Communist cause and using whatever means necessary to establish international communism, even if this meant betraying one's own country.

What Kim Philby and his friends did not see, of course—in fact, refused to see even when it was put right before their eyes—was that communism in Russia as it actually worked out, was *not* an ideal form of government. In theory, perhaps, it was beautiful in its idealistic simplicity. In reality it led not to total freedom for the Russian people but to their total oppression, an oppression every bit as bad as or worse than it had ever been under the czars.

Communism was always about to achieve its idealistic goals. But it never actually did so. Meanwhile, millions of freedom-loving people were slaughtered, and the dark night of totalitarian dictatorship settled over the country. The Soviet answer to this was that the ends justified the means. Dissidents—those who disagreed with the government—had to be eliminated to enable the true Communist state to be established. But there were always more and more dissidents to be eliminated and the freedom that was promised "tomorrow" never came.

Communism at British Universities

Nevertheless, communism was popular and fashionable in the 1930s, especially among university students at such schools as Oxford and Cambridge. The Communist International movement, or Comintern, had spread its tentacles into both the student bodies and faculties of these and many other universities in Europe as well as the United States.

At Cambridge, the Comintern had enlisted a graduate member of the faculty, Anthony Blunt, as a spy and recruiter for the NKVD (forerunner of the KGB). He had been recruited to join the Communist cause by Guy Burgess, who had left Oxford in 1934 to become part of a Soviet espionage network. Blunt taught French, but he also kept a sharp eye out for other potential Communist recruits. It was Blunt who enlisted first Kim Philby and then Donald Maclean in the Red espionage ranks. While there was little actual espionage work to be done at this time, these recruits would stand the Russians in good stead during World War II.

Blunt, perhaps encouraged by Burgess, also succeeded in enlisting an American studying at Cambridge as a potential Russian spy in 1935. This was Michael Straight, whose parents had founded *The New Republic*, an American liberal magazine which Straight later edited.

When he returned to the United States, Straight was contacted by a Soviet agent named "Michael Green," who tried to make Straight a full-fledged member of Green's spy network in Washington, D.C. This, Straight refused to do.

Graduates of Oxford and Cambridge—the two schools are frequently loosely linked together as "Oxbridge"—have traditionally gone on to attain the highest posts in British government, business, and the arts. Blunt, for example, was eventually knighted and became an adviser to Queen Elizabeth II. Maclean and Burgess became top diplomats, and Philby a top member of British intelligence. Like Philby, the other three men also worked for British intelligence during much of their careers.

Oxbridge graduates, as well as the graduates of other elite British schools, are referred to as "Old Boys." Informally, these Old Boys have always banded together to help one another succeed in business and public life. As a result, it has often been said that Old Boy networks actually rule Great Britain. This tradition was carried into another sphere of activity when Blunt, Philby, Maclean, and Burgess secretly formed what amounted to an "Old Boy Spy Network" in the service of Russia.

At Cambridge, Philby joined the left-wing University of Socialists Society, sponsored by Blunt. Here Philby became acquainted with his first Communists. Before he was graduated he became treasurer of the society. After graduation in 1933, Philby traveled in Central Europe where, he later said, he actually began his espionage work for Russia. This is perhaps true; but if so, there is little doubt that Blunt set up Philby's meetings with members of the NKVD.

Back in England, Philby became a foreign correspondent for the London *Times*. At this time there was a civil war going on in Spain in which the Communists were among those trying to defeat the Nationalist forces of General Francisco Franco. Philby managed to get himself assigned to Franco's headquarters as a war correspondent. From that vantage point he was able to report the war's progress not only to the *Times* but also, secretly, to his Russian spy masters. Russia, of course, was backing the Spanish Communists opposing Franco and was thus more than interested in what was going on in Franco's headquarters. Eventually, however, the Communists and their comrades lost the war, and Franco became dictator of Spain.

Espionage During World War II

When World War II began, Philby's Russian contact told him to try and get into the British secret service. Philby's Old Boy buddy, Guy Burgess, was already working for the British Military Intelligence (MI-6), and he was able to recruit Philby for a job in his department. It was indicative of how successfully the Old Boy network operated that Philby was accepted for a job in intelligence merely on Burgess's recommendation and with virtually no investigation (vetting) of Philby's background. This was also indicative of how much trouble lay ahead for the whole British intelligence organization.

At this time there was an NKVD (later KGB) officer working in the Soviet embassy in London. His name was Anatoli Gromov (sometimes called Gorsky). Gromov had been stationed in London since 1936, and he would remain there throughout most of the war. It was he who would direct the espionage activities of Philby, Burgess, and Maclean. Maclean had also gone to work for British intelligence at the start of the war, but not in London with Philby and Burgess. Maclean was assigned to Britain's Code and Cipher School at Bletchley Park in Buckinghamshire, and it was he who informed Stalin and the Russian military that Britain had broken the German code used to send secret military and diplomatic messages. Through Gromov, Maclean also supplied the Russians with actual decoded messages.

Meanwhile, in London, Philby and Burgess also kept Gromov supplied with so much secret information stolen and photographed from MI-6 headquarters that Vladimir Petrov, a KGB agent who defected to the West in 1954, later told his interrogators that "the cipher clerks at the Soviet embassy spent all their time relaying it by radio to Moscow, while regular diplomatic communications had to go by mail." Anthony Blunt, who had been recruited into MI-6 at the recommendation of both Burgess and Philby, was the Old Boys' photographer of documents "borrowed" for overnight study away from the MI-6 offices. The Russians supplied Blunt with a special camera for this work, and he spent many nights taking pictures from dark until dawn when Burgess and Philby had to return the documents to MI-6 headquarters. Needless to say, their Soviet spy masters were more than pleased with the volume and quality of secret documents provided by the "Old Boy Spy Network" all through the war.

Great Britain's Anti-Russian Department

Long before World War II ended, it became clear to the Allies that they would win the conflict. Like Stalin, Churchill had little faith in Russia's remaining an ally of the West much beyond the war's end. As a result, British intelligence was instructed to expand its anti-Russian department and prepare to have spies in the Soviet Union as soon as peace was declared.

When Philby told his Russian contact about this development, Gromov instructed Philby to become the head of this newly expanded department at all costs. As far as the Russians were concerned, Philby was the logical choice for this role. His intelligence-gathering efforts had at least equaled those of Burgess and Maclean, and Philby had far greater administrative abilities. Burgess was a heavy drinker, erratic and unpredictable by nature, and in any event had his eye set on a postwar diplomatic post. Maclean also was slated for the British Foreign Office, and Blunt's future was uncertain.

By means both fair and foul, Philby did exactly as Gromov had instructed. Philby's record as an intelligence officer was excellent, making him a logical candidate for the post, but there were several men who outranked him standing in his way, including his own boss, Major Felix H. Cowgill.

By using vicious gossip and ruthlessly playing office politics, Philby managed to discredit all his competitors, including Cowgill, who was rudely shunted aside. In 1945 Philby was named the head of the Secret Intelligence Service (SIS) department in charge of anti-Communist and anti-Russian operations.

Philby's Close Call

Philby had not been in his new job long when he came within a hairsbreadth of disaster. In Istanbul, Turkey, a Soviet embassy staff member who was also an NKVD agent had offered to defect to the West if both he and his wife were given asylum in Great Britain. This man was Constantin Volkov. Volkov's offer was forwarded to Philby by Knox Helm, the British ambassador at Istanbul.

Included in Helm's report was a statement to the effect that by way of proving his good intentions Volkov was ready to name three NKVD agents now working in Great Britain. Two of these double agents, Volkov said, had worked in British intelligence during the war but had recently been shifted to the foreign office. The third was a key member of Great Britain's new anti-Russian department. As far as Philby was concerned, Volkov might as well have spelled out the names of Burgess, Maclean, and Philby.

Philby immediately went into action. He consulted with the head of the British Foreign Office about a possible Russian diplomat's defection in Istanbul and said that he, Philby, would have to personally fly to Turkey to make sure the defector was not a Soviet "plant." It was a distinct possibility, he insisted, that the Russians were trying to infiltrate an NKVD mole into their midst in the person of Volkov. Then Philby requested the foreign office not to make a move about accepting Volkov's offer until Philby had a chance to check out Volkov's authenticity.

Philby's next move was to report the explosive situation to his NKVD contact in London. Philby had no doubt that Gromov would move fast in this crisis situation. For his part, Philby did not move too fast. He wanted time for Gromov to act. Fortunately—for Philby, that is—bad weather prevented his departure by air for several days, and he also experienced delays en route.

Finally, however, he arrived in Istanbul and went immediately to the British embassy, where he requested that a secret meeting be set up between him and the prospective defector, Volkov. Philby made it clear that he wanted this first meeting to be a private one, since—although he didn't say so—he feared Volkov might blurt out the three incriminating names.

Ambassador Helm agreed to Philby's proposed plan and instructed one of the British embassy aides, a man named Page, to make the contact

with Volkov at the Soviet embassy. Page had frequent need to call the Soviet embassy, so his call
would not be suspicious.

Philby remained in Page's office while he made
the call and requested to speak to Volkov. There
followed a long delay before someone came back
on the line, and then the phone went dead. A mys-
tified look was on Page's face as he turned to
Philby and said:

"They say they never heard of Volkov."

It was Philby's turn to look puzzled. But his
look was playacting. What he wanted to do was
grin happily. Gromov had done his work, and
Volkov had become a nonperson.

Mr. Philby Goes to Washington

Philby continued in his anti-Soviet role for several years, apparently to the satisfaction of his
British bosses and certainly to the satisfaction of
his Soviet spy masters, since he kept them fully
informed of all of Great Britain's intelligence and
counterintelligence activities as they related to the
Soviet Union. Then, in 1949, a real espionage
plum fell into his lap. He was posted as SIS representative to Washington, D.C. There he was to
work closely with both the FBI and CIA. His
Soviet contact in London was also delighted at the
news and assured Philby the NKVD in Moscow
would most certainly approve.

Philby's London contact was a new one, someone who had not yet been named. He replaced Gromov after the war, when Gromov followed Maclean to Washington, where Maclean was sent as a top foreign office diplomat in the British embassy. There Maclean sat in on all meetings of the Combined Policy Committee on Atomic Energy as secretary. Maclean, of course, passed on transcripts of all of his secretarial notes on vital atomic energy matters, including postwar development of the United States' growing nuclear weapons arsenal, to Gromov, who promptly relayed them to Moscow.

Maclean had been recalled to London for a new job shortly before Philby was assigned to Washington, so from the Soviet standpoint it was now up to Philby to take up providing Russia with secret intelligence information where Maclean had left off.

Burgess, meanwhile, had continued to work in the British Foreign Office in London. But Philby was not in the United States for very long before Burgess was also assigned to Washington to replace Maclean on the British embassy staff. Delighted that he and his old friend would once again be together, Philby made arrangements for Burgess to live with him in a house on Nebraska Avenue.

There were, of course, other reasons besides friendship in Philby's hospitality. He wanted

Burgess's direct pipeline to the Atomic Energy Policy Committee, and he also wanted to keep the alcoholic Burgess under control.

In his early contacts with the CIA and FBI, Philby began to hear ugly rumors—ugly to him, at least—about leaks of intelligence information to Russia from someone in the British embassy. These leaks had now stopped, but their source was still under investigation. Philby realized that the source could only have been Maclean while he was still in Washington and assumed that FBI agents would soon come to the same conclusion, if they had not already done so. But the FBI seemed to be concentrating its investigations on the embassy janitorial staff and other low-level employees who had perhaps stumbled onto secret information and sold it to supplement their small salaries.

Actually, there was one CIA staff member who was already convinced that Maclean was a Soviet spy. This agent was James Angelton, who had served in Great Britain during World War II with the Office of Strategic Services (OSS), the forerunner of the CIA. Angelton had maintained his European contacts when he continued his espionage work with the CIA after the war, and several of these contacts had named Maclean as a Soviet agent. At first, none of Angelton's colleagues took his information about Maclean too seriously, but when a list of possible suspects was compiled, Maclean's name was included on it. In a visit with a CIA acquaintance, Philby was shown this list. He knew it would only be a matter of time before the Americans zeroed in on Maclean. Maclean had to be warned.

Philby met with Gromov several times outside Washington. Gromov suggested to Philby that Burgess would be the logical person to warn Maclean, if Burgess could somehow get recalled to Great Britain. When Philby made the suggestion to Burgess, Burgess instantly agreed to make arrangements to be recalled. He did so by the simple method of getting himself arrested three times in one day for driving his high-powered Lincoln automobile at speeds of up to ninety miles per hour in the nearby state of Virginia. Although Burgess had diplomatic immunity, the U. S. State Department suggested that Burgess might be more suited to driving on British rather than American roads. He was recalled to London in May of 1951.

By this time, British authorities had been alerted by the Americans of their suspicions about Maclean. Consequently, Maclean was under so-called loose surveillance and had been briefly questioned by his foreign office superiors when Burgess arrived in London. Nevertheless, Burgess was able to see and warn Maclean, apparently without further alarming the authorities.

But a few weeks later, Burgess received a cable from Philby. It said simply that if Burgess did not make arrangements to dispose of the Lincoln automobile he had abandoned in Washington, Philby would "send the car to the scrap heap." Burgess got the hidden message.

Maclean and Burgess Flee to Russia

When he sent the cable, Philby expected that only Maclean would flee England. He did not expect Burgess to go with him and had so told his Russian contact when he suggested plans be made for "one man" to escape from London.

But in this instance, Burgess was more astute than Philby and realized that if the game was up for Maclean, it was undoubtedly up for himself and no doubt Philby as well.

Following Burgess's second warning, Maclean took the train from London to his home in Tatsfield. Burgess met him there in a hired car. To this day, authorities are not clear how the surveillance on Maclean was so loose that no one knew of these actions. In any event, from Tatsfield the two men drove to Southampton, where they boarded a ferry that landed at St. Malo in France. From there they were not heard from again until foreign newsmen reported their presence in Moscow.

At this time, former U. S. Army General Walter Bedell Smith was in charge of the CIA. Smith was

considerably more decisive than some of his counterparts in Great Britain. He put two and two together and reached the conclusion that if Maclean
and Burgess were Soviet spies, then their friend
Philby must be also. Smith promptly informed
London that Philby was no longer welcome in the
United States as a liaison between the British SIS
and the CIA.

Philby's Kid Glove Treatment

But British intelligence was far more lenient
than General Smith. In fact, many critics have
since said that the leniency with which Philby was
treated was a typical example of the worst aspects
of the "Old Boy" attitude at work.

Philby was questioned at length by his colleagues. He was even finally asked to resign from
British intelligence. But his resignation was accompanied by a "golden handshake," a handsome sum of money as severence pay. He was
never accused openly of wrongdoing and never
brought to trial. In commenting on this aspect of
the Philby case, British historian Brian Freemantle has said that one of Philby's British interrogators acknowledged, "Philby . . . . knew as
much as we did. I knew he was guilty, but I
couldn't prove it. And we're not the KGB." This
comment was evidently an implication that British

intelligence would not stoop to physical torture to make a suspect confess—especially not an "Old Boy."

Philby was allowed to go free for several years. He earned a living as a foreign correspondent for the London *Observer* and the *Economist* in Beirut, Lebanon. There he continued his work for what was now the KGB and also, unbelievably, occasionally provided British intelligence with certain secret information.

Then, in 1961, Philby was openly accused of being a Russian spy. Anatoli Golitsin, a senior KGB agent, defected to the CIA at Helsinki, Finland, and was turned over to James Angleton. He named Philby as Russia's chief KGB spy in Great Britain and the United States. Because of Great Britain's earlier lack of interest in information about Philby, Angleton was in no hurry to pass along this report. But even when he did, Harold Macmillan who was head of the foreign office (and later prime minister) openly defended Philby, saying there was no "hard evidence" against him.

Finally, however, in 1963 British intelligence sent one of their representatives to Lebanon to confront Philby with the accusations that had continued to be made against him. This man was Nicholas Elliott, a long-time friend and intelligence colleague of Philby's. Astonishingly, Philby made a full confession to Elliott. But Elliott could not arrest Philby since he had no official authority to do so. All he could do was suggest that Philby return to Great Britain—as a dutiful "Old Boy" should—and turn himself over to the authorities.

Philby Flees to Russia; Unmasking of Blunt

The next day, January 23, 1963, Philby disappeared from Beirut. He surfaced a short time later in Moscow. Not much was heard of him again for several years. But then, in 1968, his espionage autobiography was published in New York. It was entitled *My Secret War*. In it, Philby made no apologies for having betrayed his country. On the contrary, it was an arrogant, self-serving justification for all that he had done. Nevertheless, there were those who thought that one of history's master spies must be lonely indeed in his expatriate home under close surveillance by the KGB. The KGB, of course, would take no chances of Harold "Kim" Philby becoming so homesick that he might decide to defect to his true home and become a triple agent, once again the honest servant of Great Britain and the West.

Anthony Blunt, the fourth member of the Old Boy spy network, was not exposed as a KGB spy until 1979. His three Communist colleagues—Burgess, Maclean, and Philby—all maintained a discreet silence about him, and Philby made no mention of him in his autobiography. Nevertheless, there were persistent rumors about Blunt's connection with the traitorous trio, and British intelligence slowly but surely continued to investigate him. The American Michael Straight supplied both the FBI and British intelligence with information about how he had been recruited as a potential Communist spy by Blunt back in the 1930s at Cambridge University.

By this time, Blunt had risen high in royal court circles. He had long served as the surveyor of Queen Elizabeth's art collection and was now *Sir Anthony Blunt*. When Sir Anthony was confronted with all of the evidence that had been gathered against him, he, too, readily confessed to having been a secret Soviet KGB agent. Since he had apparently been relatively inactive in espionage work in recent years, Sir Anthony was not imprisoned or brought to trial. He was, however, stripped of his knighthood and relieved of his duties as an adviser to the queen. There were those, especially among the other Old Boys of Great Britain, who thought this was punishment enough. But there were those few freedom-loving dissidents who thought the punishment should have been made to fit the crime and that as a traitor, he should at least have gone to jail.

Both Anthony Blunt and Donald Maclean died in March of 1983. Blunt, seventy-five, died of a heart attack in his London apartment. Maclean, sixty-nine, who was known to have been suffering from cancer, apparently died of pneumonia. Guy Burgess had died twenty years earlier in Moscow in 1963. In late 1983, it was believed that Kim Philby was still alive somewhere in the Soviet Union.

IX

The Atomic
Bomb Spy Ring

IN THE SUMMER of 1982, a sixty-three-year-old man died in obscurity in Toronto, Canada. His death went all but unnoticed by the news media. A few newspapers printed brief stories about him on their inside pages, and a handful of television news programs included a few words about his passing. And yet at one time this man's disclosures about Russian espionage in the United States, Great Britain, and Canada had rocked the Western world.

The man was Igor Gouzenko, who back in 1945 had been listed as a cipher clerk in the Soviet embassy in Ottawa, Canada. Actually, he was an officer in the GRU. His defection to the West resulted in the unmasking of more than two dozen members of a spy ring that at least one historian, William Manchester, has called "one of the most successful in the history of international espionage."

On an autumn night in 1945, young Gouzenko stuffed more than one hundred intelligence documents under his shirt, left the Soviet embassy in Ottawa, and walked hurriedly down Charlotte Street on his way to Canadian authorities to turn himself in as a Russian defector. The documents he carried disclosed an elaborate network of Canadian, British, and American scientists, teachers, and ordinary citizens as well as foreign refugees who had been supplying the Soviet GRU and NKVD (KGB) with priceless military and scientific information, including details of the development of the atomic bomb.

Young Gouzenko's defection to the West was for purely personal reasons. He liked living in Canada. Married, the father of one son, and with his wife Anna about to have a second child, Gouzenko had been told by his boss, Nikolai Zabotin, that he was about to be recalled to Russia. Zabotin was listed on the embassy roles as a military attaché. Actually he, too, was an officer in the GRU, a colonel, and the head of a spy ring that had operated successfully for several years. The papers, 109 in all, that the defecting Gouzenko carried with him included details of the membership and operations of this spy ring.

Gouzenko had a hard time getting anyone to believe his story. First he tried to turn his papers over to a newspaper, the *Ottawa Journal*. He was told there to go to the minister of the Department of Justice. At the Justice Department building, he was told that the minister could not see him and was advised to contact the Royal Canadian Mounted Police. Finally, the Mounties took him in, listened to his story, and called in Canadian counterintelligence.

The counterintelligence agents got an earful. They had long suspected that someone was leaking Canadian information about top-secret scientific developments in radar, antisubmarine devices, and sophisticated explosives. But now they learned that their atomic energy projects at Montreal and Chalk River, Ontario, had been penetrated by Soviet agents.

Gouzenko's Disclosures

Dr. Alan Nunn May, a British scientist, had come to Canada to take charge of the Montreal atomic laboratories. Now, according to Gouzenko, it turned out that May was actually a Soviet spy known to the Russians as "Alek." While in Britain, "Alek" had spied for the Russians. In Canada he had continued his spying. This, of course, meant that the spy ring had tentacles that stretched into the United States, because

May was one of the few people fully acquainted with the top-secret American Manhattan Project—the development of the atom bomb.

By this time, all the world knew that the United States had perfected an atom bomb, since it had been used to end the war by destroying the Japanese cities of Hiroshima and Nagasaki in August, just a few weeks before Gouzenko's defection. But how the bomb was made was still thought to be top secret. Certainly no nation in the West wanted Russia to learn how the feat had been accomplished. In this, too, the West was to have a rude awakening.

Canadian counterintelligence wasted no time reporting Gouzenko's information to the FBI in the United States. And it soon developed that May was merely the tip of the iceberg. Hidden beneath the black espionage waters in America there lay a monstrous destructive force that threatened to rip the bottom right out of the ship of state.

Another British physicist named by Gouzenko was Klaus Fuchs. Fuchs's name really brought the FBI to attention. May had merely worked around the edges of the Manhattan Project from his post in Canada. Fuchs had been in on the development of the atom bomb in the United States from the very beginning.

That beginning, for all intents and purposes, was early in World War II at Los Alamos, New

Mexico. True, scientists worked at the University of Chicago to prove that the making of an atom bomb was possible, but it was at Los Alamos that an actual bomb was designed, assembled, and tested—a bomb that was first exploded at nearby Alamogordo, New Mexico.

Oppenheimer's Team at Los Alamos

In charge of the Los Alamos project was J. Robert Oppenheimer of the University of California. The FBI had always had doubts about Oppenheimer's being given this job, since he was a political liberal with many Communist friends. No hard evidence of disloyalty to the United States had ever been presented against Oppenheimer, although later continuing suspicions about him led to the removal of his security clearance.

Oppenheimer assembled a team of top-ranking physicists, including several German refugees who had been working on nuclear fission experiments before World War II began. Among these ex-Germans was Klaus Fuchs, an enemy of the Hitler regime who fled to England to escape the Nazis. Fuchs became a British citizen and this fact, plus his hatred of Hitler, enabled him to get a top-secret clearance with little or no investigation when Oppenheimer requested him for the Los Alamos atom bomb project. Actually, he was a dedicated Communist and his true loyalties were to Russia.

Once in America, Fuchs was contacted by Soviet secret agent Anatoli A. Yakovlev, who operated under cover of the Soviet consulate in New York. Yakovlev told Fuchs to work with a man named David Greenglass when he got to New Mexico. Greenglass was a U. S. Army enlisted man working as a Russian agent. He was assigned to the Los Alamos project as a machinist and had access to blueprints and other vital documents used in the development of the bomb. These, plus whatever other valuable information Fuchs could provide, were to be turned over to Yakovlev in New York for forwarding to Moscow. Yakovlev soon told Greenglass that Moscow thought the material he was providing was "extremely excellent and very valuable."

Other agents involved in the atomic bomb spy ring in the United States and for whom Yakovlev acted as a control were Harry Gold, a long-time Communist industrial spy, Greenglass's sister, Ethel Rosenberg, and her husband, Julius. Gold acted as a courier between Los Alamos, where he picked up secret atom bomb documents, and New York, where he delivered documents to the Rosenbergs. They in turn gave them to Yakovlev, who paid them handsomely. "Money is never a problem," Julius Rosenberg once told Greenglass.

The Rosenberg File

Julius and Ethel Rosenberg arranged the initial contact between Gold and Ethel's brother, David Greenglass. Later they also acted as paymasters for the spy ring with money supplied by Yakovlev. Klaus Fuchs, however, always refused to accept any payment for his espionage efforts. His betrayal of the bomb, he later said, was a matter of idealistic principle.

The Rosenbergs were to become the most notorious and controversial members of this traitorous network. The children of Eastern European immigrants, both had been born and raised on New York City's Lower East Side. As teenagers, Ethel and Julius had become friends at Communist meetings. They had been married in 1939, the same year the war began in Europe. When Ethel's brother, David Greenglass, was only thirteen years old, she introduced him to the Communist cause.

Julius Rosenberg was a graduate of the College of the City of New York, where he studied electronic engineering. He first went to work as a civilian engineer for the U. S. Signal Corps. Ethel went to work for the U. S. Census Bureau. Both later denied they were Communists who had obtained federal jobs so they could spy on U. S. government activities in preparing for war. But Julius's job enabled him to spy on East Coast defense plants. Both also later denied their participation in the atom bomb spy ring, but the evidence against them would prove to be overwhelming and both would be sentenced to death. They would be the first native-born American civilians to be sentenced by a civil court to be executed as spies.

The scientific material that the atom bomb spy ring turned over to Moscow was worth billions of dollars in money to the Russians and perhaps ten years in time. The Russians probably would have mastered the intricacies of the bomb eventually, but the material the spy ring provided made it possible for them to do so at a fraction of the cost and time they otherwise would have had to spend. The United States had used a major portion of its industrial plant as well as its industrial genius to perfect the bomb. The Soviet industrial plant, virtually in ruins because of the war, would take a decade to restore. As historian Manchester has said, "The Russians could scarcely have learned more about nuclear weapons had they been partners in the undertaking. . . . The information was beyond price." It involved charts, graphs, and formulas for nuclear fission as well as actual blueprints of the finished bomb. Before the first bomb was exploded, the Russians were able to follow every step along the way as it was built. A draftsman's sketch drawn by David Greenglass showed the bomb as it was perfected, according to a U. S. atomic expert who testified at the later trial. And when the bomb was successsfully exploded, Klaus Fuchs personally gave the Russians his eyewitness account of what the explosion had looked like and its total effects.

Interestingly, when Stalin was first given information about the beginnings of the Manhattan Project for building an atom bomb, it failed to impress him. Russia was then busy fighting a desperate battle to prevent destruction at the hands of the invading Germans, and the Soviet leader had little time for information about scientific experiments. But there were those in the Russian military forces who recognized the bomb's deadly significance and potential. That was why the military had alerted the GRU to find out as much as possible about the progress of the American atom bomb experiment.

The GRU's success in this espionage effort was also why Stalin later showed no surprise at a meeting in Potsdam, Germany, near the end of the war, when President Harry S Truman, who had become president in the spring of 1945 following Roosevelt's sudden death, announced that the U. S. had perfected an atom bomb. At the time, Truman assumed that Stalin simply did not understand the significance of the bomb. Only later would Truman realize that Stalin had not acted surprised because he had known as much about the bomb as Truman had. In fact, it is certain Stalin knew about the bomb *before* Truman did, since Roosevelt had thought the Manhattan Project so secret that he had not even informed Truman, his vice president, about it. Full knowledge of the project came as a surprise to Truman after he was sworn in, while Stalin's secret agents had kept him as fully informed as was Roosevelt.

The Canadians were the first people to blow the whistle on the atomic spies in their midst. (This information also came as a surprise to Truman.) Before they did so, however, Colonel Nikolai Zabotin, Gouzenko's former spy master and head of the GRU agents in Canada, quietly slipped out of Canada, made his way to New York, and sailed aboard a Soviet ship to Russia. He was never heard from again in the West.

Later, the Soviet ambassador to Canada, Georgi Zarubin, was also recalled to Russia. He *was* heard from again. He showed up a year later as ambassador to Great Britain!

Spy Ring Cracked in Canada

In February 1946, the Canadian government announced that a Soviet spy ring had been operating in Canada and appointed a royal commission to carry out a full investigation. Gouzenko only agreed to testify before the commission if he could wear a hood over his head and speak through a voice-distorting device to prevent his being recognized. From the time of his defection until his death from natural causes almost forty years later, Gouzenko lived in constant fear of assassination by the Russians.

In the spring of 1946, the royal commission issued its report. In all, more than twenty-five Canadians were accused of spying for the Russians. Not all were brought to trial. Several escaped to Cuba and one fled to Poland. Several were acquitted. Of the rest, all received stiff prison terms. Alan Nunn May, meanwhile, had returned to England. In 1946 he was brought to trial in London's Old Bailey and sentenced to ten years in prison. He served less than half of this sentence, however, and was released on December 30, 1951.

Reactions in the United States

In the United States, the FBI investigation of the suspects ground on more slowly. Then, in 1949, a confession by Klaus Fuchs, also in London, triggered action in the United States. Fuchs actually confessed his Soviet espionage activities to a Scotland Yard detective rather than to British intelligence. Brought to trial in Bow Street Police Court, Fuchs appeared to be, as one British reporter said, "The last man in the world you would expect to be a spy." And yet the quiet-mannered, plainly dressed Fuchs peered over the rims of his glasses and calmly admitted that "from 1943 through 1947, while engaged in government atomic work in the United States and Great Britain, I passed secret information to Soviet agents." He added, "I had complete confidence in Russian policy, and I felt no hesitation in giving all the information I had." Fuchs was sentenced to prison until 1959, when he went to live in East Germany.

During the course of his trial, Fuchs also disclosed that before he met Harry Gold at Los Alamos, he had been instructed by his control in New York to carry a tennis ball for identification purposes. Gold would be carrying a book and a pair of gloves. When Gold first contacted David Greenglass, each man carried one half of the torn top of a box of raspberry-flavored Jell-O. Gold was told to say, "I come from Julius." The two men were then to match the tops of their Jell-O box. If they fit, it was safe to carry on their spy business. The incident of the Jell-O box top was widely featured in the British and American press.

Fuchs's confession naturally led to Harry Gold and the Rosenbergs in New York, where they were then running a war surplus business. Gold confessed when FBI agents found a map of New Mexico still in his apartment that showed the routes he had followed and the rendezvous points for meeting with Greenglass and Fuchs. Gold was immediately jailed.

Greenglass was next on the FBI's hit list. Julius Rosenberg offered Greenglass and his wife several thousand dollars to escape to Russia, but they had an infant baby and refused to risk the baby's safety by becoming fugitives. They decided to remain and face the music. They, too, were soon arrested. David Greenglass was sentenced to prison and released in 1960.

Despite the fact that Ethel Rosenberg was his sister, David Greenglass implicated her and his brother-in-law in his confession. The resulting indictment against the Rosenbergs accused them of "obtaining information concerning atomic weapons, fuses, gunfire mechanisms, and other military matters," and giving this information to Russian agents. The Rosenbergs insisted they were innocent and continued to do so right up to their deaths. They were given a jury trial and found guilty in March 1951. Judge Irving Kaufman, calling their crime "worse than murder," sentenced them to die in the electric chair.

Subsequently, the United States Supreme Court denied all of the numerous Rosenberg appeals, and Dwight D. Eisenhower, who had succeeded Truman as president, turned down their pleas for clemency. They were electrocuted at New York's Sing Sing prison on June 19, 1953.

Rosenberg Protests

During the Rosenbergs' trial and for years afterward, there were numerous demonstrations in major cities throughout the United States protesting their innocence. These demonstrations were to rival in size and violence those that would come later protesting the United States' continued participation in the Vietnam War.

The protests were staged not only by American Communists spurred on by the KGB but also by non-Communist clergymen, scientists, liberals, and humanitarians. There were also those who demonstrated against the Rosenbergs, however, and carried signs reading "Kill the Dirty Spies."

On the night the Rosenbergs were executed, there were hundreds of young demonstrators outside the White House. Some of them carried placards that read "Ike's Menu: Two Fried Rosenbergers Coming Up." President Eisenhower's only comment then or later was, "I can only say that by immeasurably increasing the chance of atomic war, the Rosenbergs may have condemned to death tens of millions of innocent people over the world."

Today there are still many people in the United States who think that the Rosenbergs were not guilty and should not have died. Or, if they were guilty, others say what difference did it make? The Russians would have built the bomb anyway. Perhaps Harold C. Urey, a Nobel Prize winner in atomic research at the University of Chicago, had the best answer to that. On September 23, 1949, when it was announced that "an atomic explosion has occurred in the Soviet Union," Urey said, "There's only one thing worse than one nation having the atomic bomb. That's two nations having it."

The Rosenberg case was truly one of the most famous examples of Americans being involved with the GRU and the KGB. But it was only the forerunner of an even more celebrated case involving an American journalist, a self-confessed Soviet agent for the GRU, who accused a former top-ranking member of the U. S. State Department of also being a Russian spy. The two men were Whitaker Chambers, a former editor of *Time* magazine, and Alger Hiss, who was at the time of Chamber's accusation the head of the august Carnegie Endowment for International Peace. Interestingly, Hiss had been a U. S. delegate and secretary-general at the founding convention of what was to become the spy-ridden United Nations.

X

The Pumpkin
Spy Papers

LIKE MANY OF England's Oxbridge
students, many American college and university
students, especially along the East Coast of the
United States, became Communists during the
1920s and 1930s. They did so, again like their Oxbridge counterparts, out of disillusion with their
country's government and a frustrated idealism.
They looked to the Communist cause for a better
way of life for the American people.

One such student was Whitaker Chambers, who
later said: "The dying world of 1925 was without
faith, hope, character. Only in communism had I
found any practical answer at all to the crisis, and
the will to make that answer work. If it was the

outrage, it was also the hope of the world."

Chambers was one of two brothers who were raised in Lynbrook on Long Island, New York. His brother, Richard, became an alcoholic at an early age and later committed suicide because, Chambers said, "of his despair with the world." Chambers shared his brother's despair but thought he had found a better answer to it in communism when he became a student at New York's Columbia University. There he met his first Communists and quickly lost himself in their common cause.

Chambers soon became so involved with his newfound faith that he decided to drop out of school and devote himself full-time to what his comrades claimed was the forthcoming Red revolution. He officially joined the Communist party and began to write for its newspaper, the *Daily Worker*, as well as another leftist publication, the *New Masses*. While working for these papers, Chambers met a young woman named Esther Shemitz, who was a radical pacifist. They were married in 1931 and continued their efforts for the party as a husband-wife team.

In 1935 the Chamberses were ordered to move to Washington by the GRU. There they were instructed to begin gathering secret U. S. government information and documents to be forwarded to Moscow.

Mr. and Mrs. Chambers Meet Mr. and Mrs. Hiss

According to his later testimony before a committee of the U. S. Congress, as well as in his autobiography, Chambers and his wife became acquainted with Alger Hiss and his wife, Priscilla, soon after the Chamberses arrived in Washington. Also according to Chambers, the two families became close friends—so close, in fact, that for a time they even lived together in a modest house on P Street.

Hiss, too, was a Communist, Chambers said. More importantly, he worked for the U. S. State Department and was able to feed to Chambers all manner of classified government documents. Hiss allegedly brought this material home in his briefcase each night, Chambers would photograph either the original documents or handwritten or typed copies of them, and Hiss would return the original material to the State Department files early the following morning.

The Odd Couple

Hiss and Chambers were an odd couple to be such close friends and coconspirators. Chambers was a plain, squat and somewhat fat man, and his clothes usually looked as if he had slept in them.

He did, however, have a brilliant mind, and perhaps this is what attracted Hiss to him—if, indeed, he was attracted.

Hiss always looked every inch the perfect State Department gentleman. Tall, lean, somewhat elegant, he dressed immaculately in Ivy League clothing. Brought up in Baltimore, he attended Johns Hopkins University and then was graduated from Harvard Law School in 1929. He soon became a member of a distinguished East Coast law firm.

In the 1930s, Hiss had gone to work for newly elected President Franklin D. Roosevelt's New Deal government, serving in the State Department. Much was later made of the fact that, by "coincidence," Alger and Priscilla Hiss came to Washington in 1935, the same year that Whitaker and Esther Chambers arrived there. Hiss would remain in the State Department until 1946.

Alger and Priscilla Hiss soon became prominent members of Washington society and were listed in the *Social Register*, which was hardly apt to be a roster of Communist party members in the nation's capital. That a man from this background could even have considered joining the Communist cause, let alone enlist as a Communist spy, was beyond the comprehension of those who knew him. And that was why Chambers's accusation of Hiss as a traitor would, when it came, be such a thunderbolt.

In 1938 Chambers decided to leave the Communist party. He did so, he later explained, because he experienced a religious conversion and now saw a faith in God, rather than political beliefs, as the only solution to the world's ills. But Chambers knew that quitting the Communists was about as difficult as quitting the Mafia, the nation's crime syndicate, and that he might not live long after his resignation. As a hedge against his own assassination, Chambers gathered together microfilm copies of many of the documents Hiss had given him as well as numerous notes in Hiss's handwriting. These he gave to his wife's nephew, a Brooklyn attorney named Nathan Levine, telling him to turn them over to the FBI if Chambers should suddenly meet with a mysterious "accident."

In 1939 Chambers went back to work for *Time*, the national weekly news magazine, as a book reviewer. Soon he became a senior editor there, covering not only books but foreign news as well. And now that he was an ex-Communist, Chambers began to see the Soviet Union as a threat to the United States and other free world democracies. There were many other men and women like Chambers who had become disillusioned with communism and now denounced it. But Chambers was one of the few actual ex-Soviet spies to do so.

Hiss Rises in U. S. State Department

Hiss, meanwhile, became a more and more important figure in the State Department. During World War II he was an adviser to President Roosevelt at several meetings of the Allied heads of government—Roosevelt, Churchill, and Stalin. One of these meetings was at Yalta in Soviet Russia's Crimea near the end of the war, where it was later claimed that the United States made far too many postwar concessions to the Soviet Union. Hiss also worked closely with Roosevelt on plans for founding a world peace-keeping organization, the United Nations. The United Nations was a long-held dream of President Roosevelt's for the postwar world. He would not live to see his dream come true. But Hiss would. He would, in fact, be one of its founders and help write its charter.

After Roosevelt's death, Chambers claimed that the late president had been told during the war that there were Soviet spies in the U. S. State Department, but had refused to heed the warning. According to Chambers, Adolf Berle, Jr., who was then in charge of State Department security, had relayed this information from Chambers to Roosevelt, and Roosevelt had simply told Berle to "go jump in the lake."

As the cold war between the Soviet Union and the West developed after World War II, hunting down Communists who might still be serving within the government and acting as agents for Russia became a phobia in the United States. Heading this spy hunt, which soon turned into a witch hunt, was Wisconsin Senator Joseph R. McCarthy. One of the agencies used to try and track down these suspects was the Un-American Activities Committee of the U. S. House of Representatives (HUAC). In 1948, because of his notoriety as a reformed Red, Chambers was called before the HUAC. In his testimony, Chambers casually named Hiss as a Communist, although at this time he did not claim Hiss was a Russian GRU spy.

Hiss Denies Accusations

When confronted by newsmen and women with Chambers's statement, Hiss calmly and flatly denied that he had ever known or even heard of Chambers. Later, Hiss appeared before the HUAC and denied under oath Chambers's accusation. For a short time it seemed as if the matter might be dropped right there, but because of the national hysteria about Communists in government that was prevalent in the land, Chambers's repeated claim that Hiss was a Communist kept appearing in the news media. Finally, Hiss retaliated with a $75,000 libel suit against Chambers.

With the filing of this suit the fat was in the fire,

because now Chambers leveled the charge that Hiss was not only a Communist but a Red spy who had worked with Chambers in stealing U. S. State Department secrets and turning them over to the Soviet Union. Chambers supported his spy accusation with the documents he had given to his wife's nephew for safekeeping.

These documents were seemingly damaging enough to Hiss, but in a hearing before the House Un-American Affairs Committee, Chambers claimed he had additional rolls of microfilm that were even more damaging. Chambers said he had held these films back because they might contain material that would be damaging to other people.

Chambers was ordered to produce the microfilm, but he could not do so immediately because he did not have them available. Where were they? Chambers had resigned from *Time* magazine late in 1948 and was living on a farm in Maryland. The films were hidden there, he said. And now a truly bizarre note entered the case. Chambers's hiding place for the film, he said, was in a hollowed-out pumpkin in a field on his farm! Accompanied by a counsel for the HUAC, Chambers journeyed to the farm and produced his cache of spy papers. They were found exactly where Chambers had said they would be—in an oversize, hollow pumpkin. Their actual contents were not disclosed until somewhat later.

Enter Richard Nixon, Future President

As accusations and counteraccusations continued in the pumpkin spy papers case, Hiss
gradually backed off from his claim that he had
not previously known Chambers. A confrontation
between the two men was arranged by Richard M.
Nixon, a California congressman and future U. S.
president. Nixon was just beginning to make a
name for himself as a powerful anti-Communist
legislator, and he sensed that in the Hiss-
Chambers case he had a chance to make the name
Nixon a household word. This meeting was held
at New York's Commodore Hotel. During the
confrontation, Hiss grudgingly admitted that he
may indeed have known the man Chambers
"casually" back in the thirties—1935 to be precise—but if he had known him, he had known him
not as a Whitaker Chambers but as a journalist
named George Crosley.

Nixon promptly challenged Hiss to name three
other people who might have known Chambers as
Crosley. Hiss said 1935 was too long ago for him
to recall offhand any such names. Later, when
Hiss did provide several such names, investigators found them to be useless—the people
were either dead or could not be found.

Nevertheless, Hiss still seemed to be in the
clear. The statute of limitations had now run out

for trying anyone who might have stolen state secrets as far back as 1935.

But Nixon was not about to let Hiss off the
hook. A week later he was called to testify before
the HUAC in Washington. There, Nixon confronted Hiss with Chambers's claim that Hiss had
once given Chambers a 1929 Ford automobile for
use by Communist party members. Hiss reluctantly admitted he may have given such a car to
"Crosley." Since the title change for this car
could easily be traced, Hiss was virtually forced
into this admission. Hiss also admitted that he had
once loaned Chambers/Crosley several hundred
dollars—a princely sum during the economic depression of the thirties. This and other testimony
began to make it clear to the congressmen on the
committee that the relationship between Hiss and
Chambers/Crosley had not been quite so casual
after all.

In defending himself against Hiss's libel suit,
Chambers had to prove his previous association
with Hiss. He did so by presenting the pumpkin
spy papers on microfilm, several of which were
longhand summaries of classified State Department documents written by Hiss himself. Others
were classified documents that had been copied
on a Woodstock typewriter owned by Alger and
Priscilla Hiss. This Woodstock typewriter, or one
that was accepted in court as the one used to copy
the original documents, was later produced as

evidence. Experts testified that its keys matched the spy notes found among the pumpkin papers.

The libel case against Chambers was dismissed, and shortly afterward Hiss was indicted by a federal grand jury. The indictment was on two counts of perjury—for his claim that he had not known Chambers as Chambers, and for claiming that he had not "passed numerous secret, confidential, and restricted documents" to the Communist courier, Chambers. There was very little doubt in the public's mind that the perjury charges were actually an excuse to try Hiss for spying against the United States for the Soviet Union.

Hiss Brought to Trial

Hiss was indicted on December 15, 1948. His first trial began on May 31, 1949. It ended on July 8 when the jury could not reach a verdict. Eight jurors were for his conviction, four said Hiss was innocent. His second trial began on November 17, 1949.

During this trial, Hiss openly admitted that the handwriting in the various summaries of classified documents from among the pumpkin papers was his. Asked to explain this fact, Hiss said he frequently wrote out such summaries for other State Department officials. State Department officials denied knowing anything about such a practice. In any event, Hiss was asked, how did Chambers get hold of these summaries? Hiss did not know. He suggested, however, that someone might have taken them out of State Department wastebaskets. Then why were they all neatly folded and not wadded up into balls, as was normally the case with wastepaper notes? Hiss had no idea. Hiss, the second jury decided, had no idea about far too many things. He was found guilty, and on January 21, 1950, was sentenced to five years in prison.

After the trials, Chambers remained in retirement on his three-hundred-acre Westminster, Maryland, farm where he worked on his autobiography, *Witness*, and wrote articles for various magazines. He also became a part-time student at Western Maryland College, majoring in French. Occasionally, Chambers called upon Hiss "to speak the truth for the good of society as a whole." Chambers died on his farm of a heart attack at age sixty in July 1961. Ever the conspirator, he had made arrangements for no announcement of his death to be made until his body had been cremated.

Hiss was released from jail in the fall of 1954. He took a job as a $100-a-week salesman for a New York City comb manufacturer and was soon earning $20,000 a year. In the 1960s, he became a salesman for several stationery and printing companies. In the 1980s, Hiss was living in retirement in New York City. In occasional interviews, he steadfastly denied his guilt, insisting he had been "speaking the truth" from the very beginning. There were many who believed him, including the National Emergency Civil Liberties Committee, which spent some $1,000,000 trying to clear Hiss of the perjury charges of which he had been found guilty.

No Soviet official would ever discuss the Hiss-Chambers case or even mention either man's name. Partly because of this stubborn Soviet silence, there were persistent rumors in intelligence circles that Hiss, and through Hiss the U. S. government, had been the victims of a classic Russian espionage frame-up. It was typical, some Western intelligence experts said, of how the KGB and the GRU operated in such cases. If so, the frame-up had worked marvelously well.

XI

Tradecraft for KGB Killers

WHEN WHITAKER CHAMBERS quit the Communist party and resigned his role as a Soviet spy and courier, he feared he would be assassinated. After Igor Gouzenko defected from the GRU in Canada and broke the atom bomb spy ring, he lived the rest of his life in fear of Russian retaliation. The fact that both men apparently died of natural causes in no way proves that their fears were imaginary. There are those, in fact, who have suggested that Chambers and Gouzenko and numerous other KGB and GRU defectors did *not* die from natural causes.

As historian Freemantle has said of Soviet agents, "To defect is to die." And the Russians make every effort to live up to this pronouncement. The KGB even has a section called the Execution Action Department, or Department V, made up of trained killers to enforce it. The KGB also annually issues a book containing the names and biographies of the Russian defectors. This KGB "hit list" runs to several hundred pages. It is issued annually because each year certain names are deleted as grim proof that the KGB killers have done their job. Not always are they successful, but often enough to strike fear in the hearts of any would-be defectors. The fact that names are also added to the list each year is a mark of courage on the part of men and women who know they are risking their lives but choose to defect anyway.

As the KGB's special antidefectors department has grown and improved over the years, so have the techniques or so-called tradecraft for killing dissidents. No longer are such crude weapons as axes used to speed a dissident's departure, as in the murder of Leon Trotsky. Today, highly sophisticated techniques have been developed, so that often it is virtually impossible to detect that a victim has actually been murdered.

In the Soviet Union itself, important dissidents or would-be defectors whose sudden deaths might cause a stir in the world news media are confined to mental hospitals for "treatment." One such hospital is Moscow's Serbsky Research Institute for Forensic Psychiatry. General Petro G.

Grigorenko, a Soviet World War II hero, was confined here for his opposition to Nikita Khrushchev. Grigorenko had been a loyal follower of Joseph Stalin and when he died and Khrushchev eventually succeeded him, Grigorenko was outspoken in his criticism of the new Red leader. In the spring of 1964, Vladimir Semichastny, then head of the KGB, recommended that Grigorenko be placed in the Psychiatry Institute for "diagnosis."

At the institute, Grigorenko was asked by Dr. Margarita Taltse, a diagnostician, what he thought of Khrushchev. "Khrushchev," the outspoken Grigorenko replied, "is an ordinary zero who accidentally became the head of state. But he will not remain in power long. He'll be out by this autumn."

Grigorenko was declared insane for thinking he could "prophesy what was going to happen in the future." He was then confined to Leningrad's Special Psychiatric Hospital for further treatment.

But to everyone's surprise, especially Dr. Taltse's, Grigorenko's prediction came true. Khrushchev was replaced by Brezhnev in October of 1964. Then, everyone wanted to know how Grigorenko had been able to predict Khrushchev's downfall. Grigorenko simply maintained a wise silence, and early the following year he was pronounced "rehabilitated" and released from the hospital. Later, he defected to the West.

Dissidents Driven Mad

But usually those dissidents within Russia who are sent to special psychiatric hospitals are dealt with in a much more efficient manner. If they are not already mentally disturbed—and few are—they soon lapse into insanity. This is accomplished by administering sophisticated drugs to the "patient." For example, the Soviets have perfected one combination of drugs that will induce schizophrenia, which causes the person's personality to disintegrate so that he or she loses touch with reality. Until recently, schizophrenia has been generally regarded as a hopeless form of insanity. Such serious mental deterioration can readily lead to physical deterioration, resulting in the patient's gradual decline and death.

But it is in the tradecraft for dealing with defectors outside the Soviet Union that the killers of the KGB's Executive Action Department (or Department V) have really reached perfection. One such tradecraft device is a gun that fires a capsule of hydrogen cyanide into the victim's face; the poison gas from the exploding capsule kills him instantly. If the body of the victim of assassination by this cyanide capsule gun is not examined for an hour or so, death will appear even to an expert physician as having been caused by a heart attack.

The one drawback to this ingenious weapon as far as the assassin is concerned is that if it is used at close quarters, the killer himself or herself may also inhale some of the deadly fumes. As an antidote to the cyanide fumes, the killer is instructed to swallow a pill shortly before he attacks his victim. At first, KGB killers were somewhat doubtful that this pill would be an effective countermeasure to the cyanide fumes, but their doubts were soon stilled by the best possible means—the gun's successful use.

Murder of Rebet and Bandera

In 1957 a KGB agent named Bogdan Stashinsky was sent to Munich to kill two former political leaders who had fled from the Russian Ukraine and were now carrying on anti-Communist activities in West Germany. These two men were Lev Rebet and Stefan Bandera. They were members of the Organization of Ukrainian Nationalists (OUN), which was dedicated to regaining Ukraina's independence from the Soviet Union.

Stashinsky shadowed both of his "targets" for weeks before he succeeded in cornering each man separately and firing the explosive cyanide pellet in his face. Both deaths were publicly attributed to heart failure, but Stashinsky's control officer, Alexander Shelyepin, soon got word back to the KGB center in Moscow that the gun was an unqualified success. Shelyepin later became head of the KGB.

The West did not learn how Rebet and Bandera had actually died until 1961, when Stashinsky himself defected to West Berlin police. He was married to a German woman, Inge, who persuaded him to defect and confess to the slayings. He was given only a short prison sentence. When he was released, Bogdan and Inge Stashinsky went into hiding somewhere in the Western world. They, too, lived in constant fear of being tracked down by a member of the KGB's Executive Action Department.

Before Stashinsky's defection, however, both American and British counterintelligence agencies had learned about the cyanide pellet gun and proceeded to secretly perfect their own version of it. Tradecraft devices do not remain secrets long among the world's intelligence agencies. There can be little doubt that the cyanide gun, as well as even more sophisticated murder weapons, have been used by the West as well as by the KGB, even though there has been no hard proof of their use. Every now and again some intelligence agent dies under suspicious circumstances, apparently from natural causes, and soon the rumors about the cause of his or her death begin to spread.

Death of CIA-Agent Mulcahy

Such was the case with CIA-agent Kevin Mulcahy, who died alone apparently of causes unknown, outside a motel cabin in rural Virginia in November 1982.

Mulcahy was scheduled to testify against a former CIA agent, Edwin Wilson, who was accused of supplying guns and ammunition to various international terrorist groups around the world. Wilson had left the CIA in the 1970s and set up an arms export firm in Washington, D.C. Mulcahy had gone to work for Wilson for a time, thinking the firm was secretly being operated as a front by the CIA. When he discovered it had no connection with the CIA and was actually an international terrorism-for-hire operation, Mulcahy quit and reported his findings to government authorities. Although Wilson fled the country, he was eventually lured back and arrested, tried, and convicted for illegally trafficking in arms. Originally, Mulcahy was to be one of the prime witnesses against Wilson.

It is generally known in intelligence circles that the KGB has both sponsored international terrorism and taken advantage of it where it has occurred spontaneously. It does so because violent political unrest in a country provides fertile ground for the spread of communism. Further, one of the main countries Wilson worked with as a merchant of death was Libya. And Libya's revolutionary leader, Muammar Qaddafi, has been not only a long-time enemy of the United States but also a strong supporter of the Soviet Union. In return, the Soviet Union has supported Qaddafi both economically and in his terrorism efforts, which have included threats of assassination against the president of the United States, Ronald Reagan.

If the KGB had wanted Wilson to go free, it has been speculated, one of the best ways to assure that result at his trial would have been to eliminate the prime witness against him, Kevin Mulcahy. But Mulcahy, according to an autopsy performed after his death, had been drunk and suffering from pneumonia and emphysema.

These conditions alone, however, had not killed him. What or who had? There was no answer. And what was he doing in an out-of-the-way motel room in Virginia? No one seemed to have that answer, either, but a friend, Ray Martinez, later reported that Mulcahy had told him, "I have to be careful, because somebody will probably be out looking for me."

Mulcahy took several suitcases filled with information on Wilson when he went into semihiding at the Mountain View Motel Court in the Shenandoah Valley. There, according to the motel owner, Mulcahy spent the week before his death drinking heavily. Early one morning, Mulcahy's lifeless body was found slumped to the ground outside his motel cabin door.

Everyone involved in the case, including the FBI, insisted Mulcahy had not been murdered.

But then the FBI had also insisted that a lesser-known and anonymous witness in the case against Wilson had not been murdered, either, when his fishing boat had exploded off the Bahama Islands in the spring of 1982.

Despite the government's lack of these two key witnesses, Wilson was convicted in late December 1982 of smuggling guns to Libya. He was sentenced to fifteen years in prison and fined $200,000.

One of the truly ingenious tradecraft murder devices developed by the KGB became public knowledge in the autumn of 1978, although it had probably been used before that. It was used to kill Georgi Markov, a Bulgarian writer who had defected to the West and was engaged in anti-Communist radio broadcasts for the British Broadcasting Corporation (BBC).

Bulgaria is not a part of the Soviet Union, but it might as well be. Among the several Soviet satellite nations in Eastern Europe, it is the most loyal to Russia. Its secret police work hand in glove with the KGB both at home and abroad.

Prevented by censors from writing anything that was critical of Russia or the Russian-dominated Bulgarian government, Markov fled his native country in the early 1970s. In London, he soon began BBC propaganda broadcasts that were beamed into Bulgaria several times a day. Radio Free Europe also carried his anti-Soviet messages into other Russian satellite nations. Well known in Eastern Europe before his defection to the West, Markov was regularly listened to by a vast audience on thousands of clandestine radios. In Bulgaria alone, it has been estimated that Markov's audience numbered more than half of the nation's eight million people. Soon after Markov's broadcasts began, the KGB Executive Action Department marked him for murder. Word was passed and the means for Markov's assassination were provided by the KGB to the Bulgarian secret police.

Assassination Attempt by Umbrella

On a rainy day in the first week of September 1978, Markov was walking across London's Waterloo Bridge on his way to work. When he passed a bus queue at the far end of the bridge, a man carrying an umbrella stumbled against Markov and he felt a sudden, sharp pain in his right thigh. The man with the umbrella apologized and then jumped hastily into a taxi.

The burning pain in Markov's leg continued, and when he got to the BBC offices he told a co-worker that a man with an umbrella had stabbed him. The two men went into a washroom and examined the wound. It was small, but red and angry-looking, like a poisonous insect bite.

By the next day, Markov was running a high

fever, but the family doctor told Markov's wife over the telephone that her husband probably had the flu. Markov himself did not think so, however, and he told his wife about the umbrella incident.

Within a matter of hours, Markov became so ill he had to be rushed to the hospital. There, doctors could do nothing for him, although it soon became apparent he was suffering from a severe form of poisoning, since his white blood count was enormously high.

It was not until after his death that a metal ball smaller than a ball bearing was removed from Markov's leg. Experts were called in to examine the ball and found two pinpoint-size holes bored into it. Chemical analysis determined that inside these pinholes had been an exotic and deadly poison called ricin. Made from the castor oil plant, ricin is much stronger than cobra venom and is one of the five most poisonous substances known to science. Even if they had known what it was, doctors probably could have done little to save Markov's life.

At about the same time Markov was being attacked by the KGB agent with the umbrella in London, another Bulgarian defector was being similarly attacked in Paris. This man was Vladimir Kostov, also a radio broadcaster. Kostov had been encouraged to flee Bulgaria by Markov's propaganda broadcasts. He had fled to France where he, too, spoke out freely and publicly against Russian oppression in Bulgaria.

Kostov was not attacked by an assassin with an umbrella but by one with an air rifle. Kostov was walking near the Arc de Triomphe when he heard the crack of a gun and instantly felt a stinging sensation in his back. He was rushed to a nearby hospital, where numerous tiny pieces of metal were extracted from the skin on his back. He had been wearing a heavy woolen sweater, and apparently the tiny metal ball had fragmented before it could penetrate his body. Kostov survived the attack, but later the metal fragments were forwarded to London, where they were found to contain traces of the same deadly poison, ricin, that had killed Markov.

Assassination Attempt on the Pope

The KGB's "Bulgarian connection" was also active elsewhere in Europe. Late in 1982, evidence began to emerge that there may have been Bulgarian and KGB involvement in an attempt on the life of Pope John Paul II on May 13, 1981. In this assassination attempt, however, a plain, old-fashioned gun had been used.

Polish by birth, Pope John Paul II had been active and outspoken in his opposition to the Soviet-controlled government of Poland, perhaps

even privately encouraging a revolution there. For
this reason, it was rumored that the KGB had put
a price on his head.

Immediately after the near-fatal shooting of the
pope, a twenty-four-year-old Turkish terrorist
named Mehmet Ali Agca was arrested for the
crime. Later, Agca was sentenced to life imprisonment. During his trial, the would-be assassin
claimed he had acted alone, but once he was in
prison he began to change his story. From his account and investigations carried on by the Italian
police, the following story emerged:

Communist agents in Sofia, the capital of Bulgaria, allegedly offered Agca $1.2 million to shoot
the pope. Alleged Bulgarian agents in Rome were
said to have planned the attack and provided Agca
with a gun and a getaway car. At least one back-up
assassin would be on hand in St. Peter's Square if
Agca failed in his attempt on the pontiff's life.

Following these disclosures, a Bulgarian air-
lines official was arrested in Rome and charged
with taking part in planning the attack. Arrest
warrants were also issued for two former members of the Bulgarian embassy's Rome office who
had returned to Sofia.

As these stories became public, the Soviet
Union angrily denied any part in the attack on the
pope, saying the alleged Bulgarian connection was
an "absurd insinuation" and a "Western cam-

paign steeped in lies." Rome officials, however, described the attack as "an act of war."

In addition, Richard E. Pipes, President Reagan's senior adviser on the Soviet Union and a member of the U. S. National Security Council, said in a television interview in mid-December 1982 that it was "almost certain that there was Bulgarian and KGB involvement in the shooting of John Paul II." Asked if Yuri V. Andropov, who was the head of the KGB at the time of the attack, could have been involved in the plot, Pipes said, "Well, it could not have occurred without his authorization."

Today, of course, former KGB chief Andropov is the general secretary of the Communist party of the Soviet Union, the country's most powerful political post. Under Andropov there could be no doubt in the West that the Soviet Union would continue as a totalitarian police state, and that both inside and outside that country's borders the KGB and its "neighbor," the GRU, would have even more important roles than before.

XII

The Continuing War Against the KGB and the GRU

SINCE NKVD-CHIEF Lavrenti Beria was murdered and the Soviet secret police officially became the KGB in 1954, the organization has had half a dozen different directors. By far the most successful of them all was Yuri Andropov. In fact, he succeeded where Beria had failed, by becoming leader (as chairman, or president, of the Presidium) of the Soviet Union. He is the first Soviet secret police chief to have attained this position as the modern dictator of the U.S.S.R.

Andropov served as KGB chief for fifteen years under President Leonid Brezhnev, who succeeded Nikita Khrushchev as general secretary of the Communist party of the Soviet Union in 1964. Under Andropov's guidance, KGB agents successfully penetrated Western governments and intelligence agencies on a scale that had never before been accomplished. As a full member of the Politburo, Andropov also worked closely with Brezhnev on foreign policy matters. Brezhnev was in poor health, and he apparently looked to Andropov as his successor.

In the spring of 1982, sponsored by Brezhnev, Andropov was given further guidance through the corridors of power when he was named to the secretariat of the Central Committee of the Communist party of the Soviet Union. The Central Committee is the true source of political power within the Soviet government. Vitaly Fedorchuk, head of the KGB in the Ukraine, was then named to Andropov's former job as the national KGB director.

When Brezhnev died on November 10, 1982, Andropov was almost immediately named to replace him as the Soviet Union's top leader. Western observers were somewhat surprised at the speed with which the Politburo named Brezhnev's successor. It had been expected that, temporarily at least, several Central Committee members would jointly rule the nation until a successor could be agreed upon.

For his part, Andropov wasted no time in consolidating his position as the Soviet Union's new leader. In a surprise move, he named Fedorchuk to head the Ministry of Internal Affairs, while Viktor Chebrikov, first deputy chairman of the KGB, was named to succeed Fedorchuk. Actually, Andropov's move should not have surprised anyone. It was a shrewd one.

The Ministry of Internal Affairs is responsible for the country's uniformed police force. Its duties include criminal investigation and the operation of the nation's prisons. With Fedorchuk in charge of that aspect of the Russian home front and Chebrikov in charge of spying abroad, Andropov now had two old KGB comrades at his side. While Andropov's powers gave him virtually unlimited authority, he was now prepared for any serious Politburo infighting—as Beria had not been. One observer summed it up well when he said, "There's the national police under the control of the Interior Ministry, and the KGB secret police, and Andropov's boys are running both of them."

A Trio of Formidable Foes

Western intelligence officers recognized Andropov, Chebrikov, and Fedorchuk as formidable foes. All were seasoned, career intelligence officers. Fedorchuk had been the head of the KGB in the Ukraine before assuming the nation's top police post. He had served his apprenticeship in the NKVD under Joseph Stalin, so he was not noted for his "soft line" toward Soviet dissidents within Russia. In fact, in the Ukraine he became widely known for his brutally harsh methods of dealing with Ukrainian Nationalists, whom he regarded as "enemies of the Soviet state."

Less was known about Chebrikov except that, like Andropov, he was a "hard-liner" in his attitude toward the capitalistic nations of the West. Having served as Andropov's top aide when Andropov ran the KGB, Chebrikov was known to be every bit as knowledgeable as any man who had ever headed the KGB. About Andropov intelligence experts said, "He's the kind of person who would smile a friendly smile, shake your hand, and then walk you to the gallows." Chebrikov, they agreed, was cut from the same cloth.

These three formidable men came to their powerful new political, police, and intelligence posts at a time when Western intelligence agencies, especially those in the United States and Great Britain, were not operating at peak efficiency. In the United States, both the FBI and CIA had been considerably weakened by the Freedom of Information Act (FOIA). This had been passed by Congress during President Lyndon Johnson's administration in 1966 and greatly strengthened during and after President Richard Nixon's administration in 1974 and 1976.

While apparently striking a blow for democratic openness and freedom by preventing U. S. security agencies from operating in total secrecy, the FOIA nevertheless severely hampered clandestine operations by exposing them to the world. And without secrecy it is simply impossible for an intelligence agency to function.

Foreign Agents Use the FOIA

The FOIA required that all U. S. government agencies respond to requests from anybody in the world for formerly secret correspondence and records in agency files. Release of information was to be the rule, rather than the exception. As a result, the FBI, CIA, and the newer National Security Agency were literally swamped with requests, not only from legitimate investigative reporters but also from hundreds of curiosity seekers, who simply wanted to know "what the government has in its secret files on me." But more importantly, the KGB—through its clandestine agents within the United States—took full advantage of the FOIA to have a field day scanning formerly classified files.

In addition, the FBI and CIA were required to regularly process and occasionally ship documents to those who requested them in Communist countries! To make matters worse, the cost of processing FOIA requests have been enormous. In 1978 alone, the FBI spent more than $8 million on this task, and its FOIA staff grew from 8 to 305 people. Certainly the money and personnel could have been better used in tracking down KGB agents and their GRU "neighbors" within the United States.

During the early part of the Reagan administration, an effort was made to stem this tide of questions and responses by reclassifying old as well as new secret materials, but much damage to the effective work of the FBI, CIA, and National Security Agency had already been done.

The CIA had also been damaged by ex-agents and others who had obtained vital classified information about the CIA and published this information in articles and books. Some of this material went so far as to give the names of agents who were currently operating in specific areas of the world. These disclosures at best ruined an agent's effectiveness to the point where he or she had to be recalled to the United States. At worst, it resulted in the agents' deaths at the hands of the KGB assassins.

Both the CIA and the U. S. Justice Department did their best to end these disclosures. Lawsuits were brought against ex-agents who had published material without first having it cleared by agency officials, which is an agreement an individual makes when he or she joins the CIA. It was also made a criminal offense to publish CIA agents' names. Overseas renegades, however, who have published and continue to publish damaging information about U. S. intelligence operations and operatives, have not been so easily dealt with.

These were problems which the KGB as well as the GRU hoped would remain unsolved.

Recent KGB Activities in Great Britain

Meanwhile, in Great Britain, Prime Minister Margaret Thatcher's government continued to be plagued by the embarrassing discovery of supposedly loyal British subjects who were actively at work as KGB spies.

In mid-December 1982, the Labour Party's Home Affairs spokesman, Roy Hattersley, expressed the feelings of many Britons when he said in Parliament: "We have now had three decades of almost continued scandal and continued inefficiency in the British security service. . . . The overwhelming temptation is to sweep the inefficiency under the rug." Hattersley urged Parliament to start playing a major role in improving the efficiency of the British security services.

Hattersley's harsh words were prompted by the fact that since the end of World War II at least two dozen British KGB agents had been unmasked. These included the members of the Kim Philby ring and the atomic spy ring network, as well as George Blake, who had betrayed the secret of the Berlin tunnel and the identities of numerous British agents. Besides these, and more recently, there were the following:

A technical engineer, Brian Finney, who was

sentenced to fourteen years in prison in 1958 for disclosing radar secrets to Russia.

A Royal Air Force officer, Antony Wright, who was sentenced to three years in prison in 1959 for passing defense secrets to Russia.

A British businessman, Gordon Lonsdale, who was discovered to be a KGB "illegal" named Konon Molody in 1961 when he was unmasked as the head of a naval spy ring. He was returned to Russia in exchange for Gremville Wynne, a British agent who was captured by the Soviets in 1964.

Admiralty clerk William Vassall, who was also engaged in naval espionage. In 1962 he was jailed for eighteen years for selling defense secrets to the Russians.

A missile research technician, Frank Bossard, who was sentenced to twenty-one years in prison in 1965 for selling missile secrets to the Russians.

A shipyard employee, Peter Dorschel, who received a seven-year sentence in 1967 for trying to buy information about the U. S. missile-carrying Polaris submarines based in Scotland.

A Royal Air Force technician, Douglas Britten, who was jailed for twenty-one years in 1968 for passing secret codes to the Russians.

An ex-Royal Air Force sergeant, Nicholas Prager, who was sentenced to twelve years in prison in 1971 for selling aircraft bomber secrets to Czechoslovakia, a Soviet satellite.

An official in the foreign office, Leonard Hinchcliffe, who was jailed for ten years in 1972 for passing secret documents to the Russians.

An officer in the Royal Navy, Lieutenant David Bingham, who that same year was sentenced to twenty-one years in prison for passing along naval secrets to Russia.

The Geoffrey Prime Case

For the next decade (with the exception of the Sir Anthony Blunt case in 1979), there was relative quiet on the British home security front. Then, in 1982, a new rash of espionage cases broke out. The case that received the most attention in both Great Britain and the United States was that of Geoffrey Prime, a man who had been betraying U. S.-British communications secrets to the KGB for some fourteen years.

Prime was a former member of the Royal Air Force, which he had joined in 1956 when he was just eighteen to escape the poverty of his lower-middle-class home. In the RAF he was given the opportunity of taking a Russian language course. He was then assigned to Berlin to monitor Soviet military radio communications. In his spare time, he studied Russian literature and history and listened to Soviet propaganda broadcasts. Soon he became a convert to the Communist cause because, he later said, "It gave me something to believe in."

In Berlin he voluntarily contacted Soviet authorities and offered to work for them as a spy. Shortly afterward, KGB agents supplied Prime with a miniature camera with which he could photograph classified military material. Prime was in such a low-level job, however, that the material he could furnish the Russians was of little value. Nevertheless, they encouraged him when he was discharged from the RAF in the summer of 1968 to try and get a civilian intelligence job in England. Because of his fluency in Russian and his RAF experience, Prime soon went to work as a communications specialist for British intelligence in London.

When he got this job, the KGB supplied him with a shortwave radio and instructions on how to encode radio messages. For several years he regularly fed the Russians a modest amount of military information, none of which was of great importance. But the KGB praised and payed him well for his faithful efforts.

In 1975 Prime was cleared by his British supervisors to deal with materials of a higher security classification. The KGB's patience was about to pay off. Soon Prime was assigned to the highly sensitive Government Communications Headquarters (GCHQ) at Cheltenham, some eighty miles from London. GCHQ's function was to monitor all Soviet diplomatic and military communications throughout the world. The rapid development of satellite communications and the computerized electronic recording of all such communications had within recent years made such monitoring possible.

One of the additional major points of importance about the Cheltenham operation was the fact that it was operated in cooperation with the United States National Security Agency. This meant that a breach of its security would compromise American as well as British intelligence secrets.

Once Prime got the job at Cheltenham, he began communicating with the KGB not only by shortwave radio but also in person. He arranged to meet with his Soviet control in Vienna, taking with him various intelligence materials he had stolen from Cheltenham files. For these he was paid £810 ($1,300), which he was told was merely a downpayment; there would be much more where that came from, his KGB control assured him, and if he wanted to defect to Russia he would be given a pension and officer's rank in the KGB. Of course, he would be of more value to Russia by remaining at Cheltenham, and he was encouraged to do so. More trips to Vienna during Prime's vacations followed; on each he acted as his own courier, carrying British "most secret" materials for which he continued to be handsomely paid.

It is believed that the Russians received extremely valuable material for their money. American intelligence officials later said that Prime disclosed American and British code-breaking techniques as well as the exact location of all Allied nuclear warheads throughout the world. He is also believed to have told the Soviets on a week-to-week basis the armed readiness of every Allied military division in Western Europe.

Prime Gets "Cosmic" Clearance

Soon, Prime was given the highest possible secret clearance by the British, a clearance called "Cosmic." This enabled him to learn everything that it was possible for anyone to learn at Cheltenham and pass it along to the Russians.

But in September of 1977, when he was at the peak of his usefulness to the Soviets, Prime abruptly resigned from his job at Cheltenham. He gave no reason for doing so. During his last months there, however, he stole several hundred secret photographs and hid them. These he eventually sold to the Russians for £600 ($1,000).

After he left his intelligence job, Prime went to work driving a taxi in the town of Cheltenham. He had been married for the second time—a first marriage had ended in divorce—in June of 1977. His second wife, Rhona, later described Prime as "incredibly unhappy" and a "tortured personality."

It was during this period that Prime began to

commit a series of sex offenses against young girls. In all there were three such offenses, the last one occurring in the spring of 1982. One was against an eleven-year-old, the last two against teenagers. In none of the cases was the girl apparently physically harmed, merely forced to undress. But the girls reported the offenses to their parents, who reported them to authorities, and there was a widespread search for a man matching Prime's description. Late in April 1982, Prime was questioned by police but denied the attacks.

It was at this point that Prime apparently broke under the double burden of guilt as a spy and sexual offender and confessed his dual activities to his wife. After agonizing over what her husband should do, Rhona urged him to turn himself over to the police. He did so the next day, but confessed only to the assault on the third girl, making no mention of his spy activities.

Prime Unmasked by His Wife

Three weeks later, while her husband was still in jail, Rhona told police that Prime was also a Soviet spy. Finally, Prime himself confessed his espionage activities, and early in November 1982 he was sentenced to thirty-five years in prison as an agent for the Soviet Union. Lord Chief Justice Lane, in sentencing Prime, said he had done "incalculable harm."

On both sides of the Atlantic, the Prime case raised serious questions about British security. During his trial, for example, Prime admitted to having sent letters written in invisible ink into East Berlin. Why weren't such letters checked for invisible writing? And no one had sought to even mildly inquire about Prime's frequent trips to Europe. Prime himself admitted that security on the Cheltenham base was "a bit of a laughing-stock."

Security measures on the Cheltenham base began to be strengthened immediately after the Prime case. But everyone agreed it was like closing the barn door after the horse had been stolen. Soon questions began to be raised in Parliament in Great Britain; and in the United States, intelligence officials began to express doubts about continuing cooperation with British intelligence.

Then cooler heads began to prevail. U. S. Defense Secretary Caspar Weinberger said that Prime's acts had created a "serious breach," but insisted that they had not been "catastrophic."

Weinberger, of course, like his British counterparts, realized that any future lack of cooperation between American and British intelligence could only work in favor of the KGB and GRU. A wedge driven between the two countries' intelligence services would prove to be the most successful operation Soviet intelligence had yet run. Future cooperation was thus a necessity.

The Case of the Canadian Communist Spy

But then, just as the flurry caused by the Prime affair was dying down, another key Soviet agent was arrested in England, brought to trial in Britain's Old Bailey Court, and sentenced to ten years in prison for espionage.

This man was Hugh Hambleton, a Canadian economics professor at Laval University in Quebec.

From 1956 to 1961, Hambleton had served as an economics adviser at the headquarters of the North Atlantic Treaty Organization (NATO) in Paris, France. NATO is the alliance of Western nations formed for defense purposes and economic cooperation after World War II. Much of its continuing activity has been to present a united front against Soviet aggression.

While serving at NATO headquarters, Hambleton had removed thousands of pages of classified documents, taken them to his Paris home, photographed them with a camera supplied by the KGB, and passed the film on to the Russians. He eventually became so important to the Russians that he was given the honorary rank of colonel in the KGB, according to reliable intelligence sources.

After his service with NATO, Hambleton returned to Canada to continue his work as a professor at Laval. But he did not sever his connections with the Russians. In fact, during his trial Hambleton admitted that on a visit to Europe in 1975, he had had dinner with Yuri Andropov, then KGB chief. At this dinner, Andropov had given Hambleton a special hand-held decoding device to be used in receiving coded radio messages. What, if any, information Hambleton supplied the KGB from Canada is not known.

Finally, in 1979, Hambleton was arrested by the Canadian security service, which had received information about Hambleton's spy activities from Rudi Hermann, a KGB defector in the United States. Hambleton was later released by Canadian authorities because of "insufficient evidence." Actually, he was given immunity in exchange for information about the KGB.

Although he remained free in Canada, Hambleton was warned that he would be prosecuted if he visited Great Britain. Despite this warning, Hambleton went to England in the spring of 1982, where he was promptly arrested and brought to trial.

At his trial, Hambleton at first tried to convince the Old Bailey jury that he had actually been working as a double agent for French and Canadian intelligence, feeding the Russians "disinformation" under the direction of a French control, Jean Masson, and a Canadian, Jean Le Liberté. But French and Canadian intelligence officers said Hambleton had never been one of their agents.

Hambleton then changed his plea to guilty and was sentenced to ten years in prison.

Once again, there was a brief flurry of stories in the Western media about the breakdown in Allied intelligence security. Inevitably, this mild hysteria also soon began to die down. Although security may indeed once again have been breached—and would undoubtedly be breached again—there actually had been no real breakdown in the basic functions of Western intelligence agencies. Nor was there any hint of such a breakdown in the function of the KGB and GRU under the new regime in Russia.

Computer Technology—A New Spy Goal

Intelligence activities would continue as they had for decades, with agents on both sides of the iron curtain—which separates the Western world from the Soviet Union and its Communist satellite nations—trying to gain the advantage over one another. The only difference was that espionage had now become a much more highly sophisticated business, with an all-out attempt on the part of the KGB and GRU to steal computer and other high-technology secrets from the West. Western agents, of course, would do their best to prevent such theft.

XIII

Intelligence
Warfare of the Future

EXPERTS ESTIMATE THAT 85 percent of Western intelligence is now gathered by the kind of electronic eavesdropping that was being carried on at Cheltenham where KGB-agent Geoffrey Prime worked. Great advances in computers and other microelectronic devices made the Cheltenham satellite communications operation and others like it possible.

In addition, the computer has changed the way future wars may be fought. Computerized nuclear missile guidance systems already in use are just one example. Also in the works are aircraft computers that will perform as many as a billion separate functions simultaneously.

To date, the Russians have been running a bad

second-best in these so-called high-technological or "high-tech" areas. But with the help of several thousand newly assigned KGB and GRU "technology collection officers," the Soviets have made great strides in obtaining these secrets from the West. Most of the Soviet gains have been made by stealing the vital high-tech information and equipment. But they have also gone all out in recruiting key Western agents.

The Case of Bill Bell

One such recruit was William H. Bell, an employee of the Hughes Aircraft Company in California. Despite his loyal, twenty-seven-year employment record, Bell was living far beyond his means and was badly in debt when he met Communist agent Marian Zacharski in the late 1970s. Zacharski was a Polish spy working for Soviet intelligence. He recruited Bell simply by offering to buy aircraft secrets from him.

In 1982 the CIA issued a report on Soviet acquisition of Western technology. Between 1977 and 1980, according to this report, Bell gave Zacharski more than twenty reports on advanced U. S. weapons systems. Included were reports on the F-15 fighter plane's robotlike "look-at-shoot-down" radar system, as well as printouts on computer-assisted aircraft designs. Information given to Zacharski, according to the CIA, would enable the Soviet Union to build its own F-15-type aircraft much more rapidly than would otherwise have been possible. It also would enable the Soviets to develop countermeasures against advanced U. S. military aircraft.

Both Bell and Zacharski were eventually caught by the FBI. Bell was sentenced to eight years in prison and Zacharski was given a life sentence. During the course of his trial, Bell said that his own security clearance had never been reviewed in his almost three decades at Hughes and suggested that in the future, U. S. manufacturers of classified military equipment might want to be more security-conscious.

Since the Bell case, greater measures have been taken, but sometimes ordinary precautions have not been good enough. Such has been the case in several examples of Soviet theft of secrets by computer.

How Soviets Steal Computer Secrets

The Soviets, for example, have managed to plug their own computers into U. S. computer systems. In this way, they have been able to gain access to detailed printouts of weapons development and guidance systems as easily as if they were American manufacturers. One such instance occurred in the early 1980s when Soviet electronics experts operating in Vienna, Austria, on a worldwide network were able to link their computer to a top-secret computer at the Lockheed Aircraft Corporation in Sunnyvale, California. The CIA was successful in discovering and ending this electronic banditry.

Another KGB computer linkup was made between Vienna and an advanced installation for nuclear weapons design at Reading, England. This linkup was also discovered, but no one knows how much knowledge the Russians gained before the operation was broken up. There have been other such computer linkups and doubtless will be more in the future.

Perhaps the greatest success the Russians have had in such "high-tech transfers," as they are called, has been in the acquisition of microchip manufacturing equipment. Microchips are the tiny silicon wafers on which miniaturized integrated electronic circuits are etched. They are at the heart of all of today's computer and microelectronic devices.

Microchips are manufactured in what is called a semiconductor plant. Many such manufacturing and development plants are located in California's so-called Silicon Valley near San Francisco. As they have done elsewhere, the Russians assigned numerous KGB and GRU agents to their Soviet consulate in San Francisco. Their job has been to penetrate Silicon Valley and steal its secrets.

These agents used the indirect approach. They

recruited disloyal Americans who were willing to act as fronts for apparently legitimate companies. These "dummy" companies were then used to buy semiconductor equipment, silicon, and other material, just as any legitimate American company would do.

It was many months before U. S. intelligence learned about these "dummy" companies and was able to shut them down. Meanwhile, however, the Russians had shipped every bit of equipment, material, and scientific data they had obtained to the Soviet Union and there set up their own multi-million-dollar semiconductor operation.

Industrial Espionage

KGB and GRU agents have also been and continue to be active in industrial espionage elsewhere throughout the United States and the rest of the Western world. One of the most fertile areas is within companies that manufacture computers and other electronic devices for civilian use. Home computers, such home appliances as microwave ovens, video games, automatic automobile components—all use computerized equipment and material. Manufacturers in this highly competitive field are also engaged in research and development to get the edge on their competitors' products. Soviet agents daily engage in stealing as much of this information and actual manufacturing material and equipment as possible and shipping it to Russia.

Customs agents have seized millions of dollars' worth of classified military equipment before it could be shipped out of the United States. But unclassified electronic devices continue to be sent abroad. And the Russians do not always ship this material directly to the Soviet Union. Much is sent to other countries and forwarded to Russia from there.

The American intelligence services as well as the federal government have become seriously alarmed about this high-tech "brain drain" from the United States. The CIA has made presentations to the U. S. Congress, citing the country's continuing technology losses, and the U. S. State Department has requested special action to bring such losses to a halt. Even the U. S. president has been urged into action.

As a result, U. S. Customs launched "Operation Exodus," which successfully seized more than $50 million worth of unclassified electronic material at ports of exit during 1982. The CIA and FBI have both trained special counterintelligence agents to deal with high-tech theft by the KGB and GRU. At President Ronald Reagan's request, the U. S. government banned shipments of all high technology not only to the Soviet Union but also to any of its satellites. Export licenses to other countries sympathetic to the Russians are now issued with great care, and permission for the export of technological material is not permitted. Much vital high technology continues to be smuggled out of the country, however.

High-Tech Thefts Abroad

As the American crackdown has continued, Soviet agents have stepped up their activities elsewhere. Other NATO countries have been invaded by an army of undercover KGB and GRU high-tech spies. And Japan, one of the world's most successful high-tech nations, has become a new Russian prime target.

Each of these countries in turn has responded to a greater or lesser degree to try and protect its own high-tech secrets, for all of these countries' leaders know that the world of the future will be a computerized world. There are those who think that in this future computerized world there will be no place for the old-fashioned, cloak-and-dagger agent—that he died in the cold, gray dawn of the computer age. He was killed, these observers say, not by another agent but by the transistor, the miniaturized circuit, and the silicon microchip—the scientific discoveries that made the computer revolution possible.

But others have doubts about the secret agent's demise. Just as computers cannot think for themselves, so no nation's intelligence agency can be run electronically without a thinking human being directing its actions and counteractions. It is more than probable that no matter how far advanced the intelligence battles of the future may become, there will always be a KGB or GRU agent fighting on one side and a Western agent on the other. Each, of course, may be carrying a hand-held computer as he or she goes into action. But it will be the individual, human agent who will supply the computer's input.

Bibliography

Barron, John. *KGB*. New York: Reader's Digest Press, 1974.

Conquest, Robert. *The Great Terror, Stalin's Purge of the Thirties*. New York: Macmillan Co., 1968.

Dulles, Allen W. *The Craft of Intelligence*. New York: Harper and Row, 1963.

Freemantle, Brian. *KGB*. New York: Holt, Rinehart, and Winston, 1982.

Gehlen, Reinhard. *The Service*. New York: Popular Library, 1972 (paper).

Goldman, Eric F. *The Crucial Decade*. New York: Alfred A. Knopf, 1956.

Grigorenko, Petro. *Memoirs*. New York: W. W. Norton and Company, 1982.

Hood, William. *Mole*. New York and London: W. W. Norton and Company, 1982.

Manchester, William. *The Glory and the Dream*. Toronto, New York, and London: Bantam Books, 1975 (paper).

Martin, David C. *Wilderness of Mirrors*. New York: Harper and Row, 1980.

Myagkov, Aleksei. *Inside the KGB*. New York: Ballantine Books, 1981 (paper).

Penkovskiy, Oleg. *The Penkovskiy Papers*. New York: Avon Books, 1966 (paper).

Philby, Kim. *My Silent War*. New York: Grove Press, 1968.

Powers, Thomas. *The Man Who Kept the Secrets*. New York: Alfred A. Knopf, 1979.

Salisbury, Harrison E., ed. *The Soviet Union*. New York: New American Library, 1968 (paper).

Straight, Michael. *After Long Silence*. New York and London: W. W. Norton and Company, 1983.

Tolstoy, Nikolai. *Stalin's Secret War*. New York: Holt, Rinehart, and Winston, 1982.

U. S. News and World Report. *Famous Soviet Spies*. Washington, D.C.: U. S. News and World Report, Inc., 1973.

Index

About the Author

During World War II, Don Lawson spent three years overseas in Great Britain and on the European continent with the counterintelligence branch of the Ninth Air Force. Since then he has maintained a keen interest in and has written several books on various aspects of wartime intelligence activities. He also has a war library of several thousand volumes.

He has a Doctor of Literature degree from Cornell College in Iowa and attended the University of Iowa's Writers Workshop. He is also the former editor-in-chief of two encyclopedias for young people—*Compton's* and *The American Educator*. He now devotes all of his working time to writing books for young people.